HURON COLLEG

6V

ECUMENICAL STUDIES IN WORSHIP

No. 12

WORSHIP
AND CONGREGATION

by

WILHELM HAHN

*Professor of Practical Theology
in the University of Heidelberg*

translated by

GEOFFREY BUSWELL

LUTTERWORTH PRESS

LONDON

ECUMENICAL STUDIES IN WORSHIP

General Editors:

J. G. DAVIES, M.A., D.D.
  Edward Cadbury Professor of Theology and Director of the
  Institute for the Study of Worship and Religious Architecture
  in the University of Birmingham

A. RAYMOND GEORGE, M.A., B.D.
  Principal, Wesley College, Headingley, Leeds

Advisory Board:

PROFESSOR OSCAR CULLMANN
  Universities of Basel and the Sorbonne

PROFESSOR H. GRADY DAVIS
  Chicago Lutheran Seminary, U.S.A.

DR. F. W. DILLISTONE
  Dean of Liverpool Cathedral, England

PROFESSOR ROGER HAZELTON
  Dean, Graduate School of Theology, Oberlin College, Ohio,
  U.S.A.

PROFESSOR J. KUMARESAN
  Gurukul Lutheran College, Madras, India

DR. R. STUART LOUDEN
  Kirk of the Greyfriars, Edinburgh

PROFESSOR ROBERT NELSON
  Graduate School of Theology, Oberlin College, Ohio, U.S.A.

CANON D. R. VICARY
  Headmaster, King's School, Rochester, England

CONTENTS

FIRST PUBLISHED IN ENGLISH 1963
© GÜTERSLOHER VERLAGSHAUS. GERD MOHN, GÜTERSLOH 1959
ENGLISH TRANSLATION © 1963 LUTTERWORTH PRESS

This book is a translation of Wilhelm Hahn, *Die Mitte der Gemeinde: Zur Frage des Gottesdienstes und des Gemeindeaufbaus*, Gütersloher Verlagshaus, 1959.

*Printed in Great Britain by
Latimer, Trend & Co. Ltd., Plymouth*

ABBREVIATIONS

RGG: *Die Religion in Geschichte und Gegenwart*

ThBl: *Theologische Blätter*

ThLZ: *Theologische Literaturzeitung*

TWNT: *Theologisches Wörterbuch zum Neuen Testament*
                  (ed. G. Kittel)

ZThK: *Zeitschrift für Theologie und Kirche*

The references to Luther's *Werke* are to the Weimar edition. Passages from Karl Barth's *Church Dogmatics* are quoted by permission of the publishers of the English translation, T. & T. Clark of Edinburgh.

PREFACE

MANY PEOPLE TODAY are concerned with the questions of worship and the building up of the Christian community. In recent years much thought has been given to these problems, and important books have been written about them. This present work is based on these discussions, and aims to carry them further. Its special purpose is to draw out the implications of the theology of worship for the actual ordering of the Sunday service and for building up the life of the congregation. This does not mean that we shall try to indicate the way to achieve an ideal form of worship or of congregational life, an ideal form that is theologically correct and in keeping with the requirements of the age. This would be a

> misunderstanding of the task of theology, which springs from a misunderstanding of Christian worship. Christian worship by its very nature does not arise from an academic theological construction, but is an event in the actual life of the Church, when the Lord, acting through the Holy Spirit, meets His people in Word and Sacrament. Its liturgical form therefore is the fruit of the faith and obedience of Christian people. . . . The theology of worship provides the critical canon by which the particular historical form taken by Christian worship can be tested and judged. In relation to the liturgy, it has a critical function, not a constructive, creative task. As far as practical directions for the correct ordering and conduct of services are concerned, it points out the ways that are open to the Church in its worship (J. Beckmann).

This present work follows these lines. It is addressed to the theologian who is concerned with the theology of worship, to the minister who is commissioned with the task of conducting worship, and also to the Church member who is engaged in the worship of his own Church. By bringing out the nature of Protestant worship, its purpose is to show how it can be celebrated in the freedom of the Gospel, but at the same time with a sense of responsibility for seeking the most appropriate form for it to take. To speak of freedom and responsibility seems to suggest a tension between the two, but in fact the problems involved can be solved only by taking the two into consideration. The

7

solution of these problems is a task that constantly confronts all those who take part in worship. It is our hope that this work may help those who read it to render their service of worship in freedom and in obedience.

WILHELM HAHN

Heidelberg

INTRODUCTION

IN RECENT YEARS there has been evidence in the Church of a very lively interest in the question of worship. In many respects the Ecumenical Movement and the Liturgical Movement run on parallel lines, although they are by no means identical. The Liturgical Movement in the Roman Catholic Church has many points of similarity with that in the Protestant Churches, and there has been considerable cross-fertilization of ideas. The Liturgical Movement has had a far-reaching effect upon the life of local congregations; it has created a wholesome dissatisfaction with things as they are, and has had very practical results which are making the life of the Church today very different from what it was in past generations.

The Liturgical Movement would not have proved such an effective force were it not for the fact that it grew out of the great theological revival which began after the first world war. This revival brought about a new realization that the Church lives by Word and Sacrament. At the same time the rediscovery of the Biblical concept of the Spirit showed how questionable was Liberalism's separation of content and form, of spirit and matter.

In Germany it was the Church Struggle that finally brought home to the Church this realization and created a new understanding of the message of the Word and of the forms that the Word is seeking to create in the life of the Church. In addition there was the actual experience that the congregation lives by its worship of God, and that this is the focus of all its energies. From this experience two basic facts have emerged, which are accepted by all who have a sense of responsibility for the welfare of the Church, whether they favour liturgical worship or not:

1. The life of a Christian congregation and its worship must be brought into the closest relationship with one another, for its worship, in which the Word is proclaimed and the Sacraments are administered, is the life-giving centre of the congregation.[1] This fact must find

---

[1] Karl Barth describes worship in this way. Cf. *Church Dogmatics*, IV. 2, p. 638. Cf. also (*ibid.*): "It is not only in worship that the community is edified and edifies itself. But it is here first that this continually takes place. And if it does not take place here, it does not take place anywhere."

9

expression also in the organization of the Church's life, in the ordering of its ministries and particularly in the way in which the minister fulfils his official duties.[1]

2. The form of the service of worship is not an unimportant matter. On the contrary, the task of determining its form—a task which is inescapable, as the Church has, and must have, its worship—is one which must be performed by the Church seriously and with a sense of responsibility.[2] The special difficulty of this task is that whilst the purpose of the form of a service is to assist the proclamation of the Word and the administration of the Sacraments, and thereby in turn to assist in building up the congregation, which means that it must therefore be suitable for this most important function of the Church's life, at the same time there is no final form for the Church's worship on earth, nor can there be, such as could become legally binding.[3] The Church must be free in her search for the most suitable form, and it is of decisive importance for Protestant worship that this freedom should be preserved. Peter Brunner has expressed this problem of the form of Christian worship very succinctly: "We must give due weight . . . both to the *freedom* of those who are bound to the Gospel, and to the *bondage* of those who are set free by the Gospel."[4] The recognition that the centre of the Christian community is its worship confronts us with a twofold question: What is the best form for its worship, and how can the worship and the life of the congregation be related to one another?

The first fact that must be borne in mind in seeking an answer to these two questions is that they can be answered only in the light of the nature of worship, or in other words, in the light of what God is doing

[1] Cf. Karl Barth, *op. cit.*, p. 698: "From this centre of its life there can and must and may and will be also true Christian being and action on the circumference, in the Christian everyday. From it there can and must and may and will be general law and order. Thus from its liturgical root Church law must be understood as a law which (1) is ordered by divine service; (2) is continually to be found again in it; and (3) has itself the task of ordering it."

[2] We find Luther already dealing with this problem, as, for example, in his commentary on Genesis: "When we assemble for worship in Church we should not behave as though we were in the tavern or at the fair, but with propriety and seriousness." Quoted O. Mehl, *Das Liturgische Verhalten*, 1927, p. 5.

[3] This idea of "suitability" is used particularly by P. Brunner, in *Der Gottesdienst an Sonn- und Feiertagen*, 1949, pp. 19 f. and Zur Lehre vom Gottesdienst der im Namen Jesu versammelten Gemeinde, in *Leiturgia I*, pp. 279 ff.

[4] Peter Brunner, *Der Gottesdienst an Sonn- und Feiertagen. Untersuchungen zur Kirchenagende*, I. 1 (1949), p. 18.

by means of Word and Sacrament. The form of a service is merely the instrument to serve the purposes of proclamation and of the Sacraments, and thus of the congregation. But at the same time we must remember that the congregation has to be seen in the light of its worship, not the worship in the light of the congregation, despite the fact that the congregation is the creation of the Holy Spirit through Word and Sacrament. A Church's worship is not primarily something contrived by the worshipping community, but is the place where God seeks to speak and act through the proclamation of His Word—though not exclusively here. This theological insight must be maintained in relation to the Churches in Germany, although we must not in any way overlook or misunderstand their special problems. Section VII of the *Augsburg Confession* and sections VII and VIII of the *Apology* encourage us to believe—and this we must never abandon—that the actual Church, that is, the congregation that assembles for worship, is the Church of Jesus Christ, even though this is in no way identical with the official, constitutional Church and congregation. It is of great importance that we should treat questions of worship, liturgy and the building up of the congregation in the light of this insight of faith. It is therefore not only the correct approach from the theological standpoint, but is also of great practical relevance for the life of the Church and for the way in which the minister fulfils his duties.

This particular insight highlights two aspects of the problem we are considering, which are being keenly discussed at the present time by those concerned with these matters. On the one hand there is the question of the correct liturgical form of the service. We have already suggested that this must be in keeping with the nature and purpose of worship, which only faith can perceive, but at the same time the Church must be left free to seek and practise any particular form. This makes it impossible to set up the liturgical form of a service as such as a shibboleth of correct worship, or to declare that either a full order of service drawing on the riches of traditional Christian worship or an austere order with little of liturgy or congregational participation is the only right form. Article VII of the *Augsburg Confession* excludes this possibility, by making the true Church and worshipping congregation dependent solely on the pure proclamation of the Gospel and the administration of the Gospel Sacraments, and by specifically distinguishing these from the ceremonies which are "man-made". Whilst the purity of the proclamation of the Word and its corresponding Sacraments are of vital importance for Christian worship, the particular form given to it is a secondary matter. This does not mean it is an unimportant matter, but it is not central. It would lead to a complete perversion if this peripheral matter were put in the centre, for it is only by maintaining this sense of proportion that our evangelical freedom can be preserved in this question of the liturgical forms of worship.[1]

The other aspect which is to the fore at present is the question how worship can be made effective and what are the best methods whereby a service can be made to appeal to a congregation, and be made the centre around which a well-organized Church life can revolve. It is obviously not unimportant, whether the worship which a minister conducts attracts a congregation or empties the building. An absent congregation presents a serious challenge to the worship of the Church concerned, for worship is meant to "build up" the congregation, and it is for this purpose that it comes together (I Cor. 14: 26). The impression the service makes on the participants—on the active Christians as well as those "on the fringe"—also cannot be ignored (I Cor. 14: 23 ff.). But the questions what is correct Christian worship, and how worship can avoid being dismissed as a spent force and continue to be the life-giving centre of the congregation, can be answered neither by an inquiry into what the potential participants would like, nor by mere reorganization, however well planned and carried out. The former method would subject worship to men's arbitrary choices, and the latter would result in a busy, but empty and lifeless, round of activity. A dead service can be revitalized only from that which is its true centre and essence. The only service that can ever become the centre of the community is that in which God Himself declares His Word through the power of preaching, in which the central act is God's own act in the Sacrament, for which the congregation prepares itself, and in which the liturgy is the expression of a receptive faith.

A service which in this way draws its life from its centre will not make it unnecessary either to consider the views of the congregation—to which it is quite entitled—or to re-organize the life of the congregation, but on the contrary will give these activities new meaning. Worship is like a spring of water to which men can be brought in the confidence that they will find there what they really need. The congregation, its minister and its governing body all have their contribution to make if the service of worship is to be seen as the centre of the Church's life. Here again, however, a right sense of proportion

[1] I hope soon to publish a further study of the problem of liturgical form, in which these matters will be more fully discussed.

must be preserved, for the only person who will have the strength to stand firm when outward success and popular support are denied him is the one who understands that the essence of worship is to be found in the disclosure of the Word of God.

The special meaning that worship has for the Christian community has been given classic expression by Karl Barth, and I can do no better than quote his words in full.

> In divine service there takes place that which does not take place anywhere else in the community. In divine service the sabbath intervenes between six working days on the one side and six more on the other. In it it exchanges its working clothes for its festal attire. It is now an event as community. Unpretentiously but distinctly it stands out from the secularity of its environment in which it is for the most part submerged. It now casts off the anonymity of that which is distinctive and common to it; the occasional and haphazard and private character elsewhere assumed by its manifestation. It now exists and acts in concrete actuality and visibility as the congregation to which many individuals—each from his own human and Christian place in dispersion—come together to one place at one time in order that together, occupying the same space and time, they may realize the *communio sanctorum* in a definite form.
>
> There can be no doubt that not merely their life in the world, but their own everyday life as Christians as it was lived yesterday and will be resumed to-morrow, is now left behind. There can be no doubt that the hour for which the conspirators otherwise wait in dispersion has now struck, even if only provisionally and not definitively. The dimension which embraces individual Christians and Christian groups is now visible to themselves, and in their common action to the world around. This is the distinctive feature of this action within the wider context of the life of the community; the feature by which it is distinctly shown to be the centre of its life, not to be confused with the everyday either of the world or of Christians. It is shown to be its centre because here—and in this way only here—the community exists and acts in direct correspondence to its basic law, in a particular and not merely a general historicity. In divine service it becomes and is itself a witness to its own being, to its determination in the world, to the factuality of its existence. And in divine service it exists and acts prophetically in relation to the world to the extent that in divine service—and here alone directly—there is a serious discharge of its commission to be a provisional representation of humanity as it is sanctified in Jesus Christ.[1]

[1] Karl Barth, *Church Dogmatics*, IV. 2, pp. 697 f.

I

GOD'S SERVICE TO US

1. *Worship as God speaking to us and our response*

IN HIS famous sermon at the consecration of the Castle Church at Torgau in 1544 Luther expressed briefly and most forcefully the nature of worship: "My dear friends, we are now to bless and consecrate this new building to our Lord Jesus Christ. This is not a matter that concerns me alone, for you too ought to take the sprinkler and censer, to ensure that this building is erected for no other purpose than that our Lord Himself may speak to us through His holy Word, and that we in turn may speak to Him through our prayers and hymns of praise."[1] These words contain three fundamental assertions:

1. Worship is a twofold event, or in other words, it is an event with two subjects: God acts towards us, and we answer Him through what we do. This means that worship has two sides which, though they can be considered separately, must be seen in relation to one another.

2. The initiative in this event lies with God. He is the primary subject. Worship is first and foremost God's service to us. It is an action by God, which is directed towards us. Our activity in worship can be nothing other than reaction and response, the consequence of God's activity. The two sides in worship are therefore in no sense equal; they cannot even be considered as the two poles of worship, for they are essentially different.[2]

---

[1] *Werke*, 49, 588. We could also take as a starting-point Luther's explanation of the first Commandment in his *Large Catechism*, as he sets out here as well what true worship is. Cf. Vilmos Vajta, *Luther on Worship*.

[2] We shall return to the question of how the relationship between these two sides in worship is to be determined in the section "Our service as response and co-operation". How this relationship is determined is decisive for Protestant worship. On this aspect, cf. K. F. Müller, Die Neuordnung des Gottesdienstes, in *Theologie und Liturgie*, pp. 208-61. Also Karl Barth, *The Knowledge of God and the Service of God according to the Teaching of the Reformation*, pp. 191 f.: "*A sacrament according to the definitions of the ancient Church, which all agree on this matter, and hence according to the Scottish Confession also—a sacrament is an action in which God acts and man serves, his service taking the form of the*

3. What happens in worship, as far as its content is concerned, is that God speaks personally to us and that we speak to Him in reply. When He speaks to us through His Word, it is in the fullest sense what Scripture and the Reformation mean by the Word of God.

The Age of Enlightenment, which had lost sight of the Biblical meaning of this concept, could cite these words of Luther in support of its limited understanding of worship. For the Enlightenment, worship was nothing more than instruction about God,[1] instead of God's revelation and communication of Himself to His people, and their response of faith and service in the sacrifice of praise.

These words of Luther are specially valuable for our times. Under the influence of secularism and of a world in which only rational thought seems to have a place, it is hard for us to grasp the profound statements concerning worship in the New Testament. We can understand more readily this simple statement, which in fact says no less. At the same time it helps us to understand the rich descriptions of Christian worship such as we find in Revelation, in the early Christian hymn in Phil. 2: 5 ff. and in the Epistle to the Hebrews, when we realize that they are in fact covered by this simple definition of Luther's. The statements in the New Testament merely unfold from different angles what is involved in God's speaking to His people and their response. Fundamentally, therefore, it is immaterial whether we consider the question of worship in terms of Luther's words or of the fuller statements in the New Testament. As far as content is concerned, they convey the same.

The distinction that Luther draws between God's action towards us and our response to Him in worship has been adopted as the pattern in several important discussions of the nature of Christian worship and of what takes place in it.[2] As this distinction corresponds to the basic execution of a divine precept. In accordance with this precept and by means of definite concrete media witness is borne to God's grace and through this men's faith is awakened, purified and advanced. In principle this is all that can be said not only about the sacraments in the narrower sense of the term, but about the *church service* in general. The first point to which we shall give prominence is that the church service is *Divine* action."

[1] For the attitude to preaching in the Age of Enlightenment, cf. A. Niebergall, Die Geschichte der christlichen Predigt, in *Leiturgia II.* 1954, pp. 306 ff., and M. Peters, *Der Bahnbrecher der modernen Predigt. J. Lorenz Mosheims Homiletische Anschauungen dargestellt und gewürdigt*, 1910.

[2] See K. Barth, *The Knowledge of God and the Service of God*, pp. 188–216; Vilmos Vajta, *Luther on Worship*; Peter Brunner, Zur Lehre vom Gottesdienst der im Namen Jesu versammelten Gemeinde, in *Leiturgia I*, pp. 194–267.

structure of Christian worship, our discussion also will follow the same lines.

2. *The presence of Christ in worship*

To say that God speaks to us through His Word means that He comes to us, and when He comes to us in the Gospel He comes to us in Jesus Christ. The main service that God renders us in worship, therefore, is that He reveals Himself and gives Himself to us in Jesus Christ. God's presence is not limited to worship, for He comes to us in many different ways; but He has explicitly promised to be present through Christ when in worship His Word is proclaimed and the Sacraments instituted by Christ are administered. "God is present in two ways: the one is natural, the other spiritual. . . . We can say therefore He is present even in the midst of hell, death and sin . . . but He is present spiritually only where He makes Himself known, that is, wherever His Word and Holy Spirit are, wherever there is faith and worship," says Luther.[1] Jesus' words to His disciples reveal the heart of Christian worship: "For where two or three are gathered together in my name, there am I in the midst of them" (Matt. 18: 20). This promise is the basis of all Christian worship.

Worship therefore presupposes that people come together "in the name of Jesus". This formula, "in the name of Jesus", is not used with a very precise connotation in this passage, and simply means that Jesus is the cause and ground of people's coming together.[2] There is no mention of the other external circumstances of worship. The question of the number of the worshippers, and the question as to whether they are entitled to participate by virtue of their official status and ordination, or on ethical or religious grounds, are quite clearly excluded. Neither is the place of assembly for worship a vital matter, therefore there can be no question of special cultic centres. All that is of decisive importance is the promise of the presence of Christ.

This presence is a sheer gift. It can be neither contrived nor enforced by man. Neither the assembling of the congregation, nor even the proclamation of the Word or the administration of the Sacrament should be thought of as a means of procuring this presence. The presence of Christ is therefore neither an *opus operatum* effected by the Church, nor is it an *opus operantis* in the sense of being dependent on the faith of Christian people, on the subjective attitude of those

[1] Luther, *Werke*, 19, 197, 18.
[2] See Hans Bietenhard, art. ὄνομα in *TWNT*, V, p. 270.

who participate in the service. The coming of Christ is the fulfilment of the promise He Himself made, which he brings about through the Holy Spirit when and where He wills (cf. *Augsburg Confession*, V).[1]

This freedom which Christ maintains, whilst it deprives the Church of any power of disposal over His presence, does not leave the worshipping community in any uncertainty. On the contrary, there is nothing more certain than His promised presence. It is the same certainty as holds good in regard to the presence of Christ in the Sacrament, for it is a presence grounded in the unconditional saving love of God. The Christian community has good cause to lay claim to this presence and to hold on to the fact of which this promise assures us. Whoever proclaims the Word from the pulpit, administers the Sacrament, or leads the liturgy at the altar or in the midst of the congregation, should never lose sight of the "EST" of Christ's promised presence, just as Luther at the Colloquy about the Lord's Supper at Marburg wrote in chalk on the table in front of him the word "EST".

The awareness of this real presence of Christ is found throughout the New Testament. Schniewind, for example, writes in exposition of Matt. 18: 20, "This saying could be used as a motto for all the Gospels, for the words and deeds of Jesus were reported only because it was believed that the exalted Christ was present in the midst of the community when His words and deeds, His life and death, were remembered".[2] When we study the writings in the New Testament, we do not find anywhere a doctrine of the real presence of Christ in worship; but this presence is a matter of such immediate awareness that it is constantly coming to the fore in different ways.

We usually associate the real presence of Christ with the *Lord's Supper*, and it is indeed here that we have the most direct witness of it. This fact is grounded in the words of institution of the Supper, which the New Testament traces back to Jesus Himself, and which in their fourfold, though varied, tradition formed the centre of the celebration of the Lord's Supper even in the early Church. This supports the argument recently set out by H. C. Schmidt-Lauber, that the whole of the later liturgical growth, as regards the Lord's Supper at least, should be

[1] On this section, see *Apology*, Art. IV, 41–63, on the relation between *promissio* and *fides*. For Barth's definition of the relationship, see *Church Dogmatics*, I. 1, pp. 266 ff.

[2] J. Schniewind, *Das Evangelium nach Matthäus* (*N.T. Deutsch*, vol. 2, 1937), p. 195.

considered as a development of the *verba testamenti*.[1] According to Günther Bornkamm the words of institution are not merely interpretative, as are the words spoken at the Passover meal, for in the Lord's Supper they "signify a direct assertion of that which is offered".[2] It is not a question of association by analogy, but by identity.[3] The idea expressed in the *verba testamenti* points to a sacramental communion. "To this extent the dogmatic concept of the real presence . . . is quite appropriate."[4] They who celebrate the Lord's Supper participate in the Body and Blood of Christ; but it is not a question of a substance that is imparted, but of the incarnate Person of Christ.[5] In the Lord's Supper He Himself is in the midst of the congregation. He is present as the dying Lord, who gives His life for us, for the broken Body and the shed Blood are as it were a paraphrase for His death.[6] In this way the Crucified Lord is present with His people.

The particular form of the *verba testamenti* brings to light the fact that Jesus, the Crucified Lord, is not merely present, but also active, in the celebration of the Supper. This central passage of the Christian liturgy has come down as direct speech, in the first person singular, with the result that Jesus Himself appears as the speaker. Without raising here the question of the historicity of the words of institution, and bearing in mind that the *verba testamenti* have been inserted into a narrative framework which conjures up the historical context of the institution on Maundy Thursday,[7] it is important to see that when the Supper is being celebrated, and in particular at the liturgical recitation of the *verba testamenti*, the congregation hears Christ Himself speak and is made contemporary with the act of institution itself. The faithful have always rightly felt that these words spoken in the first person singular are the words of Jesus Himself speaking here and now. The narrative framework testifies to the fact that the speaker is the One who is about to enter upon His Passion, whilst the words of institution,

[1] H. C. Schmidt-Lauber, *Die Eucharistie als Entfaltung der Verba Testamenti*, pp. 125–204.

[2] G. Bornkamm, Herrenmahl und Kirche bei Paulus, *ZThK*, 1956, p. 329.

[3] *ibid.*, p. 330.

[4] *ibid.*

[5] *ibid.*, p. 331. Cf. R. Bultmann, *Theology of the New Testament*, I, p. 147.

[6] J. Behm, art. αἷμα in *TWNT*, I, pp. 173 and 175.

[7] This is not to be taken as implying any judgment concerning the controversial question of the original time of the first Lord's Supper.

by the form they take, show that the same Jesus is the One who is active in the present.[1]

The whole of the New Testament, however, does not suggest any contrast between the Crucified and the Risen Lord, but sees them both as one. The answer to the question whether it is the Crucified or the Risen Lord who is present is, therefore, that the two cannot be separated. It is Luke in particular who brings out the fellowship with the Risen Lord that is experienced in the meal, in his Easter narrative (Luke 24) and also in Acts (1: 4; 10: 41). The rejoicing that prevailed at the celebration of the Lord's Supper in the early Church springs from this fellowship with the Risen Christ, of which the community was certain, even though He could not be seen. The *Maranatha* of its eucharistic liturgy was its joyful greeting to the Christ who first came in the flesh, who was to come again, and who made Himself known and gave Himself afresh at every celebration of the Lord's Supper.

> The coming of Christ into the midst of the community gathered at the meal is an anticipation of his coming to the Messianic meal and looks back to the disciples' eating with the risen Christ on the Easter days. In the Book of Revelation, which, as we know, correlates the present service of worship and its fulfilment in the events of the last days, Christ says: "Behold, I stand at the door and knock. If any man hear my voice and open the door I will come in to him, and will sup with him and he with me." That is the answer to the old eucharistic prayer: *Maranatha! The prayer is fulfilled already in the community's celebrations of the Lord's Supper.*[2]

We can say therefore that in the Lord's Supper the experience of the community is that Christ, the Crucified and Risen Lord, and the One who is to come again, comes into the midst of the congregation, acts as Host at the meal, and with it gives Himself.

The presence of Christ, however, is by no means restricted to the Lord's Supper. It manifests itself differently, but with no less intensity, through *the preaching of the Word*. In this connection H. Schlier points out the significance of 1 Cor. 14: 25, where Paul is speaking about the service of the Word and is considering the impression made by the various kinds of proclamation on one who is "unbelieving and unlearned". When such a person hears prophesying, which broadly corresponds to what we know as preaching, "he will fall down on his

---

[1] See R. Prenter, Die Realpräsens als Mitte des christlichen Gottesdienstes, in *Beiträge zur historischen und systematischen Theologie. Gedenkschrift für D. W. Ehlert*, 1955, p. 316.

[2] O. Cullmann, *Early Christian Worship*, p. 16; cf. also p. 71.

face and worship God, declaring that God is among you indeed".[1]
Schlier translates the "in you" by "among you", which are interchangeable from the linguistic point of view, and by doing so brings
out the real meaning of the passage. The presence of God is made
manifest by the "convicting" word of proclamation, which reveals the
secrets of the heart, as it is set forth in the service. This makes a man
bow in adoration before the presence of God, and confess: He is here,
in the midst of the congregation.[2] It is a universal conviction of the
early Church that Christ Himself speaks through the mouth of His
preachers (Rom. 15: 18; Luke 10: 16).[3]

It is only the examination of the Synoptic Gospels by Form Criticism that has made it possible for us to see fully how forcefully the
presence of Christ makes itself known in the earliest proclamation.
Form Criticism recognized that the Synoptic Gospels do not claim to
give historical accounts of the life and ministry of Jesus of Nazareth,
but that they are to be understood as a collection of early Christian
sermons and sermon material.[4] The majority of the narratives are
either parts of sermons or summaries of sermons, and have therefore
grown from a context of worship. Of many of these passages it is true
to say that "each one in itself contains the person and history of Jesus
in their entirety".[5] They bear witness to Jesus not as a figure belonging
to the past, but as One present here and now. "To the original Christian tradition Jesus is not in the first instance a figure of the past, but
rather the risen Lord, present with his will, his power and his Word. . . .
The interest of the Church and her tradition do not cling to the past,
but to today."[6] Günther Bornkamm illustrates this very effectively
with reference to the passage concerning the Stilling of the Storm. He
points out that whereas Mark 4: 36 ff. directs our attention essentially
to the event concerning the Lake of Gennesaret, Matt. 8: 23 ff. shows
Jesus as the Saviour of His Church in the storms of history.[7] What

---

[1] H. Schlier, *Die Zeit der Kirche*, 1956, p. 262.

[2] *ibid.*, p. 264. E. Käsemann also says that the acclamation in 1 Cor. 14: 25 is
the congregation's recognition of the manifestation (*RGG*, 3 ed., II. p. 993).

[3] See Erich Cohen, Unsere Predigt als Christusverkündigung, in *Monatsschrift
für Pastoraltheologie*, 1958, pp. 177–88, esp. p. 180, where references to other
literature will be found.

[4] M. Dibelius, *From Tradition to Gospel*, 2 ed., pp. 9–36, 287 ff. Cf. G. Bornkamm, *Jesus of Nazareth*, p. 16.

[5] G. Bornkamm, *op. cit.*, p. 25.   [6] *ibid.*, p. 16.

[7] G. Bornkamm, Die Sturmstillung im Matthäusevangelium, in *Wort und
Dienst, Jahrbuch der Theologischen Schule Bethel*, 1948, pp. 49 ff.

Jesus was and did then in Palestine, He is and does today wherever His people gather around Him.

Thus by listening to the word of proclamation the congregation becomes contemporary with the Jesus Christ to whom the Gospels bear witness, and not merely with the Teacher before His death and resurrection, for in all these stories Jesus comes into the midst of the community as the Crucified and Risen Lord. The early Church in its preaching avoids the danger that the presence of the Exalted Christ might become a mere shadow or symbol by identifying the Exalted Lord with the historical Jesus to whom the Gospels bear witness. Through the preaching of the Word the Exalted Christ comes into the midst of the worshipping congregation as a living and authentic figure, with all the clear-cut features of the historical Jesus.

M. Kaehler has pointed out that the account of the sufferings, death and resurrection of Jesus occupies a disproportionately large place in the Gospels, with the result that they can be described as "Passion stories with a full introduction".[1] The account of the Passion, in contrast to the other sections of the Synoptic Gospels, which were made up of short and originally separate passages and sayings, is a carefully constructed unity, which must have had its place as such in the worship of the early Church.[2] There the story of the Passion and of Easter was related as a whole, and soon of course read aloud. It still finds its place in our services, and at Passiontide and Easter these passages should be included.[3] The significance of this recital of the events of the Passion and of Easter in early Christian worship is the same as what we saw to be the significance of the Lord's Supper, namely that it bears witness to the fact that the Crucified and Risen Lord is present. In the sermon He is "set forth crucified" before the congregation (Gal. 3: 1). Some manuscripts add crucified "as though He were in the midst of you", which is what we find in Luther's version. Preaching makes His cross and resurrection the real centre of the congregation. The account of a meeting for worship in the early Church which we find in Acts 4: 24 ff. gives an impressive picture of this sense of the immediate presence and activity of the Crucified and Exalted Lord.

[1] M. Kaehler, *Der sogenannte historische Jesus und der biblische Christus*, new ed., 1953, pp. 59 f., n. 1.

[2] See M. Dibelius, *op. cit.*, pp. 178 ff., and Gottfried Schille, Das Leiden des Herrn. Die evangelische Passionstradition und ihr "Sitz im Leben", in *ZThK*, 1955, pp. 161–205.

[3] The new *Agende für evangelisch-lutherische Kirchen und Gemeinden*, 1957, moves in this direction, though not clearly enough.

O. Cullmann has tried to demonstrate that one of the main aims of the Fourth Gospel is to show the connection between the worship of the early Church and the life of the historical Jesus. Although his general thesis has by no means been universally accepted, some of his main arguments certainly carry great weight. He argues that the Gospel brings out the complete identity of the Lord who is present in the early Christian congregation and of the historical Jesus.[1] "The implicit assumption of this Gospel is that the historical events, as here presented, contain in themselves, besides what is immediately perceptible, references to further facts of salvation with which these once-for-all key events are bound up."[2] These further facts of salvation are preaching and the Sacraments, and it is through these that the Christian community sees itself linked with the coming of salvation in Christ. "The presence of Christ among his people is actualized in the service of worship," especially in the Sacraments.[3] The essential point for John is that "all worship that is founded on Christ is founded on Christ's death and resurrection, and makes these events present".[4] Cullmann traces this through many of the episodes in the Gospel, and finally discusses the spear-thrust in the side of the crucified Christ (19: 34). The incident is of great importance in John's account, "because it is a very striking sign of the connection between the death of Christ and the two sacraments".[5] This connection is in the first place one of content, "in the sense that Christ gives to his Church in the two sacraments the atonement accomplished in his death. It is also to be understood chronologically, however; scarcely is the historical Jesus dead . . . when he shows in what form he will from now on be present upon earth, in the sacraments. . . ."[6] According to Cullmann, therefore, the Fourth Gospel bears witness to the immediate presence of Christ in the service. It is the special feature of John's account of Christ that it gives us this unified picture of the historical Jesus, the risen Lord and the One who is present to faith in the midst of His people.

This presence of Christ with His people, which is fulfilled primarily through the proclamation of His Word and through participation in the Sacrament, is not restricted in the New Testament to Word and

[1] O. Cullmann, *Early Christian Worship*, pp. 37-8.

[2] *ibid.*, p. 56.

[3] *ibid.*, p. 58.

[4] *ibid.*, p. 73.

[5] *ibid.*, p. 114. For a quite different view, cf. R. Bultmann, *Theology of the New Testament*, I. p. 142.

[6] Cullmann, *op. cit.*, p. 115.

Sacrament. We need only recall, for example, the meaning that Paul attaches to the Christian's fellowship of suffering with Christ.

Finally it must be stressed that the real presence of Christ is limited in two ways. On the one hand it is an invisible presence, and on the other it is an incomplete presence, which will not be complete until the Parousia. The presence of Christ in worship is hidden under the signs of Word and Sacrament, the authority of which is confirmed by the fact of their institution by Christ and by the witness of the Holy Spirit; yet to men's eyes they appear quite inadequate for the claim they make. The human weakness of the preacher and the earthly form of the Sacrament, which links it with similar phenomena in the history of religion, seem to be incompatible with the presence of Christ, although at the same time they are signs of His compassionate condescension to our world.

The human frailty of worship and of preaching can be a source of scandal and difficulty. The Christian has to learn that it is true even of worship that "we walk by faith, not by sight" (2 Cor. 5: 7), and that "we have this treasure in earthen vessels, that the exceeding greatness of the power may be of God, and not from ourselves" (2 Cor. 4: 7). It is also true that the fellowship with Christ that He now grants is not the final and complete fellowship. It is still threatened by the "wiles of the devil". It is always possible that it may be broken by weakness and sin, and that a Christian or a congregation may fail to attain the goal (1 Cor. 10: 1 ff.; Rev. 3: 14 ff.; Acts 5: 1 ff.). The Church must never lose sight of the fact that, despite the blessings of salvation already bestowed upon her, she is still *in via*, which means that she is still under the Cross. If anyone imagines he has already reached the goal, he is deluded and is in great danger (Phil. 3: 12 ff.; 1 Cor. 4: 6 ff.).

The Church therefore reaches out in joyful expectation towards the promised goal of a perfect life in the constant presence of God at the Parousia (Rev. 21). The fact that the Church is always looking towards this goal prevents her from feeling secure in a false sense of possession and from thinking that in her worship she has something that is final and complete; in other words, it prevents her from making an idol of her cultus. Instead, she is called upon to offer her worship in the same spirit in which Israel used to celebrate its Passover: "And thus shall ye eat it; with your loins girded, your shoes on your feet, and your staff in your hand: and ye shall eat it in haste: it is the Lord's passover" (Exod. 12: 11). Christians too cannot and should not linger over their cultus, nor should they settle down comfortably in their worship, for

24

it is here that they are called upon to go forth to meet their coming Lord. The cry *Maranatha*, which sounds through the eucharistic celebration of the early Church (1 Cor. 16: 22; Didache 10: 5), and which is taken up mightily in the vision of the end of all things in the last chapter of the Bible (Rev. 22: 18 ff.), reveals a Christian worship, the goal of which is the Parousia. It is not yet the marriage, but the time in which the bride adorns herself and rises to meet the Bridegroom (Rev. 22: 17).

3. *The ministry of Christ present through the Holy Spirit*

The Person and the Work of Christ cannot be separated. Wherever Christ is present, He does His Work. In worship He does it through His Word, for "God is the God of the Word, which means that He is the One who has spoken to His children".[1] In fact Luther can go so far as to say that God Himself is the Word.[2] In Christ we see the God who reveals Himself, the God who speaks to us. "The means whereby God has revealed Himself is the Word, which includes both preaching and worship."[3]

The whole of worship therefore can be included under the Word, the Sacrament as well as preaching, for these are simply two different forms in which both gift and Giver are identical.[4] The chief criterion that Luther lays down in *Von Ordnung des Gottesdienstes* is

> that everything that is done in the service should serve the purpose of allowing the Word to have free course. . . . It is better to neglect anything rather than the Word. And we can do nothing better than proclaim the Word. The whole of Scripture teaches that the Word should be given free course among Christian people. Christ Himself says "but one thing is needful", that Mary should sit at Christ's feet and hear His Word daily, for this is to choose the good part, which cannot be taken away. . . .[5]

The Word reveals the works of God:

> By means of the Word the works done by God in the past are rescued from history and made contemporary. The Word brings home these events generation by generation to all those who hear the Word. . . .[6]

[1] V. Vajta, *Die Theologie des Gottesdienstes bei Luther*, p. 119.

[2] *Werke*, 12, 107, 26.

[3] Vajta, *op. cit.*, p. 119.

[4] K. Barth, *Church Dogmatics*, I., 1, pp. 61 ff.; G. Harbsmeier, *Dass wir die Predigt und sein Wort nicht verachten*, p. 41.

[5] *Werke*, 12, 37, 56.

[6] Vajta, *op. cit.*, p. 123.

> Until the return of Christ is the era of the Holy Spirit, who brings the salvation of Christ to all nations through the preaching of the Word. . . . *Usus facti* is therefore simply . . . preaching, which is nothing less than saving history summed up in the Word. From this it follows that whenever the Word is given "free course" through public preaching, there God's mighty acts are set in motion.[1]

If we go on to ask what is the inner work that the Christ who is present in the service accomplishes in the congregation and in the individual Christian, Luther's answer is that this is the work of the Holy Spirit. In both the Large and Small Catechism (in explaining the Third Article) Luther puts in a nutshell what it is that takes place when the congregation assembles and the Gospel is proclaimed and the Sacraments administered. "The Holy Spirit accomplishes sanctification by means of the communion of saints, that is, the Christian Church. . . . He first brings us into the holy fellowship of the Church, so that there He may preach to us and bring us to Christ."[2] All true worship is the work of the Holy Spirit. It is through the Holy Spirit that God sanctifies. As the word "sanctification" means little to people nowadays, it will be more helpful if, with the aid of the leading ideas in the explanation of the Small Catechism and against the background of the New Testament, we consider the event we call worship as the activity of Christ present with His people. To look at worship in this light can be of particular assistance to the minister who has to conduct a service, as it helps him to keep in view what is the purpose of God's activity in worship, and in this way to understand better his own part in the service.

Luther teaches that through the Gospel the Holy Spirit summons, assembles, enlightens and sanctifies the Christian community and maintains it in Christ in the one true faith, and that in this community He freely forgives sins daily to all who believe. This in fact fully describes the activity of the Christ who is present in worship, if we bear in mind that the battle against the Devil and sin, to which we shall refer later, is the negative side of worship, of which we are now considering the positive side.

One might question whether the *summons* is part of the activity of Christ in the service, or whether it should not rather be thought of as something that precedes it, as missionary preaching or personal appeal

---

[1] *ibid.*, p. 127.

[2] Luther, *Large Catechism*, 3 art., 37, in *Die Bekenntnis-Schriften der ev.-luth. Kirche*, II. 1930, p. 654.

to those who are not yet believers. Cullmann draws a sharp distinction between the missionary preaching and the worship of the community: "The missionary preaching of the Apostles, which naturally did not take place within the framework of a Lord's Supper, has nothing to do with the worship service of the community."[1] Cullmann shows that there was such a thing as a service of the Word which served a missionary purpose, but that its aim was the conversion of the heathen, not the edification of the community, although this does not exclude the possibility that occasionally an unbeliever may have been present when the community assembled. It is certainly true, as 1 Cor. 10: 14 shows, that in the normal service the Lord's Supper was at the centre, and that the proclamation of the Word also had its place. But it is obvious that the New Testament provides no justification for drawing sharp distinctions here (and it should be noted that it is interpreting Cullmann's argument too narrowly to conclude that in the early Church every gathering for worship consisted simply of the Lord's Supper).[2] There seems to be no trace in the early Church of any secret discipline, for unbelievers were allowed access. The ideas employed in the New Testament to describe preaching and worship draw no distinction between proclamation within the congregation or without. In both cases it is the *kerygma* that is announced, the Gospel of Jesus Christ. It was no doubt adapted to the religious and cultural assumptions of the hearers, as we can see from the structure of the sermons in Acts, and also from the varying emphases in the picture of Christ presented by the different Synoptic Gospels; but the content of them all is the one Gospel of Christ.

All preaching, whether within the community of believers or without, is a summons. "Sanctification is therefore nothing other than bringing men to Jesus Christ."[3] The Gospel which stands at the centre of the service is not a secret doctrine, but good news for all the world. It therefore needs to be proclaimed publicly. It transcends all boundaries.[4] Luther describes preaching as *vox clamans in deserto et vocans ad fidem infideles*[5]. A service is the place where the Gospel is proclaimed, and from where it spreads out into the world. The fact that this is the

[1] O. Cullmann, *Early Christian Worship*, p. 28.

[2] See W. Bauer, *Der Wortgottesdienst der ältesten Christenheit*.

[3] Luther, *Large Catechism*, in *Die Bekenntnis-Schriften der ev.-luth. Kirche*, II. 1930, p. 654.

[4] Cf. G. Friedrich, art. κηρύσσω in *TWNT*, III, p. 712.

[5] *Werke*, 12, 211.

content of Christian worship prevents the latter from ever becoming an introverted cultic assembly. All true Christian worship is open to the world, for it reaches out to the world. It calls men out of the world to Christ, and it proclaims Christ in His ministry for the world and as Lord of the world.[1] For this reason Christian worship has to be directed to both believers and unbelievers, for it has a message for both. The fact that believers, subject as they are to the temptations of the world, still remain sinners, means that the two cannot be sharply distinguished. Luther makes this point in the preface to his *Deutsche Messe*, where he insists that the service should be "a public inducement to faith and to the Christian way of life".[2]

By summoning, the Holy Spirit seeks at the same time to *assemble* the congregation. In the New Testament this is expressed in two ways. In the first place, he who hears the call of Christ and comes to faith in Him is incorporated into Christ. In other words, out of the hearing of the Word and out of fellowship with Christ in the Sacrament there grows the body of His Church (1 Cor. 10: 17; 12: 13). The Christian no longer thinks of himself as an individual, brought into a personal relationship with Christ by his faith, for he knows that he is joined and pledged to the Church as a whole. In the second place, this means that everything in the worship of the community must be done with a view to the edification of the community (1 Cor. 14: 26). Edification includes everything that furthers the orderly and harmonious service of God and of one another in worship. Luther gives classic expression to this idea:

> I believe that there is on earth a holy community of saints, under one Head, Jesus Christ, called together by the Holy Spirit, in one faith and of one mind, with many different gifts but united in love, without parties and divisions. I myself am a part and member of this community, sharing in all the blessings that it enjoys, brought into its fellowship through the Holy Spirit and incorporated into it through hearing—and still hearing—the Word of God, for this is the only way of entry into the community.[3]

This means that worship involves in the first place assembly, and then incorporation into the people of God, in other words, being called to the mutual responsibility and fellowship of the Church. At the same time it brings the glad awareness of being sharers in the unsearchable riches which Christ has given to His people. We can say therefore that

[1] Cf. G. Friedrich, art. εὐαγγέλιον in *TWNT*, II, pp. 712, 722, 727 ff.
[2] *Werke*, 19, 75, 1.
[3] Luther, *Large Catechism*, op. cit., p. 657.

in worship the Holy Spirit creates fellowship among Christians and bestows His gifts upon them.

Among these gifts there is God's plan of salvation as revealed in Christ, the deposit of which we find in the record of revelation, the holy Scriptures. God had disclosed His secret in Christ, but it is the very nature of this secret that, despite its disclosure, it never loses its secrecy, never becomes the possession of men, and can never be fully known.[1] Yet it is one of the main functions of Christian worship that in it this divine secret, God's saving purpose in Christ, His will and His gracious commands should constantly be declared afresh. Worship is meant to *enlighten* the Christian. Thus we find that one of the marks of proclamation in the New Testament is the emphasis on instruction. We read of Jesus that He departed "to teach and preach" (Matt. 11: 1).[2] The content of His preaching, as it emerges from the Gospels, is both invitation and instruction, with a considerable emphasis on instruction. In the Pauline letters also we never find an invitation which is not at the same time instruction, in this case theological doctrine. This element of instruction, which appeals to men's power of reasoning and which furthers and deepens the understanding of the congregation, is an essential part of Christian worship. It is inevitable that a congregation will suffer greatly if this element, which gives substance to the preaching, is not given its due place. But sound doctrine must never be exchanged for the private notions of individuals (Col. 2: 1 ff.). The doctrine which edifies the congregation is always that which is tied to Scripture or inspired by Scripture, which helps the congregation to grow in the knowledge of God and in understanding (Eph. 4: 11 ff.).

The fact of *sanctification* is most clearly expressed in the New Testament in Paul's teaching that through Baptism the Christian is crucified with Christ and rises again (Rom. 6: 3 ff.; Col. 2: 10 ff.), and that in the Lord's Supper he is brought through the cup into fellowship with His blood, and through the bread into fellowship with His body. This means that through the two Sacraments the Christian directly participates in the death of Christ. But we must note that Paul says the same about preaching, for it also leads to being crucified with Christ and to the new life of faith, in which Christ Himself becomes the determining factor in the Christian's existence (Gal. 2: 19 f.). The implication of all this is that through Sacrament and Word, which are the focal points of worship, the Christian participates directly in the fate of

---

[1] Cf. G. Bornkamm, art. μυστήριον in *TWNT*, IV, pp. 823 ff.
[2] Cf. H. Rengstorff, art. διδάσκω in *TWNT*, II, pp. 141 ff.

the Christ who is now present. To stand in the presence of this Christ has its implications for a man's whole life, and has far-reaching consequences. It leads to such an intimate fellowship that a man can no longer order his own life, but must surrender his body and his whole being as a sacrifice to God. This complete sacrifice of himself is the Christian's true worship. It delivers the Christian from that "conformity to this world" which drives him into league with the forces that are opposed to God, and brings about an entirely new pattern of his life with Christ, in which the determining factor is the will of God (Rom. 12: 1 f.). Christian worship is the place where this saving work of God, which embraces a man's whole being, begins. Our worship therefore must not lose sight of this aspect, for it must help the Christian to recognize when God is requiring him to make a decision, and what the will of God for him is in the present moment.

When Luther states that the task of the Holy Spirit is to "*uphold*" the Christian "in Jesus Christ in the one true faith", he is at the same time making it clear why it is necessary for the believer to attend worship. The person who has come to faith through the appeal of the Gospel, and has been enlightened by preaching and the study of Scripture, cannot (even with this grounding) maintain his faith in the midst of the world except by the constantly renewed operation of the Holy Spirit. The forces of this world are so powerful, and the assault of the demonic powers which attack the Christian and the Church is so insidious, that it is necessary constantly to renew one's contact with the Gospel. This contact is not of course limited to worship in the narrower sense, but can be maintained by private study of Scripture, by prayer, or by recalling words of Scripture or extracts from the liturgy or the catechism. When thought of as being complementary to worship, such things can be an enrichment, but as a substitute for taking part in worship, which may not be possible for external reasons, they are for exceptional circumstances and can never be entirely satisfactory by themselves. It is by the proclamation of the Word and by the Sacrament administered in the fellowship of the congregation that the Christian lives the life of faith, for Word and Sacrament together provide the sustenance of his life with Christ.[1] We can say therefore that, in the wisdom of God, worship has this pastoral function of maintaining the faith of believers. The Holy Spirit upholds us in Jesus Christ in the one true faith and prevents us from succumbing to temptation, unbelief and doubt.

[1] Cf. G. Friedrich, art. κηρύσσω in *TWNT*, III, p. 711.

In conclusion Luther stresses particularly the *forgiveness* that is granted us in the worship of the congregation: "In the Christian fellowship God day by day freely forgives all my sins and those of all believers." In the *Large Catechism* he writes: "We also believe that in the Christian Church we have the forgiveness of sins, the assurance of which is given to us through the holy Sacrament and absolution, and in the many words of comfort throughout the Gospel. This is what we are to preach concerning the Sacraments, and this is the sum of the whole Gospel and of all the offices of the Christian Church."[1] For in spite of our faith "we are never without sin, so long as we are still in the flesh. . . . Therefore the life of the Church is so ordered that men may day by day receive the forgiveness of their sins through the Word and through signs, to console their conscience and be a comfort to them during their earthly pilgrimage. The work of the Holy Spirit therefore . . . is to bring God's forgiveness to us and help us to forgive one another, bear one another's burdens and assist one another. But outside the Christian Church, where the Gospel is not heard, there can be no forgiveness, just as there can be no sanctification either."[2]

In other words, the Christ who is present in worship always bestows afresh through Word and Sacrament and through absolution that which is the heart both of preaching and of the Lord's Supper: God's forgiving grace. The purpose of worship, therefore, is to impart this greatest gift. It is meant by God to be an inexhaustible source of life.

Our account, however, would be incomplete if we did not refer to the fact that Christ's work in the congregation does not proceed quietly and without contradiction. Christ's work is a battle, a battle with the Devil for man.[3] He makes His attack against all the bastions of the Devil and against all the evil fetters in which man is held fast. This means that in worship, where the Word is addressed to him, a man is at the focal point of this battle. When the Word lays hold of him, a man not only comes to believe, but the evil spirits also become active and the forces that are in opposition to God are set in motion. This is the special danger for man and for his worship, that the latter can only too easily turn into its opposite and become the battle-ground of the forces opposed to God, in which case it is perverted into idol worship. Such perversion does not take place when man's opposi-

---

[1] Luther, *Large Catechism, op. cit.,* p. 658.
[2] *ibid.*
[3] Vajta, *op. cit.,* p. 21, quotes Luther to this effect. See also G. Wingren, *The Living Word,* 1960, pp. 42 ff., 50 ff., 164 ff.

tion to God becomes conscious and active under the Word, for this is the inevitable result of the proclamation of the Law (Rom. 7: 7 ff.), but rather when man boasts of his achievement in worship while turning a deaf ear to God's demands (Jer. 7: 1 ff.) or when he distorts the Gospel, which is God's offer of Himself, into the law of human works and claims made upon God. This is an experience that is always coming to the Christian Church, that there is a polarity between the service of God and the service of sin, just as between the Word of God and sin, with the result that the service of God can turn only too easily into its opposite.[1]

The effect of the Word of God upon man is that man is drawn into the battle that Christ wages with the Devil. It is not the preacher who wages this battle in worship, but Christ who does it through His Word. If the minister were called deliberately to wage this battle it might easily have unfortunate results. As it is Christ who fights, both the battle and its outcome are hidden from the eyes of men. The conflict is not restricted to worship, for Christ was "manifested, that he might destroy the works of the devil" (1 John 3: 8). Sin perverts the whole of life, and Christ seeks to deliver man in every part of his life. Therefore His activity cannot be thought of as effective only within, or through the agency of, the Christian community; still less should it be thought of as restricted to the time and place of the service.

4. *The gift of fellowship in worship*

We have already pointed out that when Christ calls men into fellowship with Himself, He brings them together in His Church. We must now look more closely at the fellowship that is thus created.

We can speak of two dimensions of the fellowship that is bestowed in worship, of a vertical and a horizontal.[2] The former arises from the fact that Christ gives Himself to man through Word and Sacrament and thus draws him into personal fellowship with Himself in which he can now live the life of faith; the latter is the fellowship that arises from the fact that Christ immediately makes the believer a member of His community and thereby joins him to the whole of His community and to every other Christian. In so far as Christ Himself in His reconciling and redeeming work is associated with all men, and not only those

---

[1] It is a mistake to infer from this that there is a particular sinfulness attaching to worship or cultus, as does Harbsmeier, *op. cit.*, p. 12.

[2] Karl Barth also employs this image of the vertical and the horizontal. Cf. *Church Dogmatics*, IV, 1, pp. 643 ff.

who are Christian, which means that from His side a relationship is established even with unbelievers, so also the Christian who belongs to Christ is associated not only with his fellow-Christians, but must also turn to those who are outside the Christian Church. The vertical dimension of fellowship with Christ and the horizontal fellowship of Christians with one another cannot be separated.

Just as this fellowship with Christ is an object of faith which cannot be demonstrated or made visible, but can be apprehended only on the basis of God's promise, so also the fellowship of Christians with one another in Church and congregation is an object of faith. The Christian often seems to lose the sense of fellowship with Christ amidst the trials, doubts and temptations of life, and the same is true of the fellowship of the congregation. At times the Christian feels that he is not being upheld by this fellowship, feels that he is forgotten, and begins to doubt its reality. It is the minister in particular, as he strives to create such fellowship, who is liable to despair when his efforts seem to fail. Then he has to remind himself that the fellowship of faith is in the first place Christ's gift and is therefore something that can be perceived only by faith, and that cannot be confirmed or measured by observation. But just as fellowship with Christ manifests itself by the visible signs of Word and Sacrament, the fellowship of the congregation also has its visible marks, the most obvious one of which is the coming together of the two or three in the name of Jesus. Only if we begin with faith in the fellowship of the body of Christ, which is His gift to His people, shall we come to know fellowship on the horizontal plane, but not if we try to organize it or try to give a psychological or phenomenological account of it.

The two dimensions of fellowship are interdependent. The vertical dimension is a personal relationship in which the individual is accepted in all the uniqueness of his personality, which, far from being extinguished, comes to its full development only as it becomes aware of its responsibility over against its Creator. To this extent one might speak —though in a very different sense—as does C. G. Jung, of man's self-realization and "individuation". This self-realization bestowed by Christ is not nullified by being incorporated into the body of the Church, for the fellowship of the congregation does not involve a levelling of the personal element. The Church is not a collective which obliterates all differences and suppresses the uniqueness of the individual, but a body made up of different members, the unity and richness of which consists in the co-ordination of many individual persons. The

fact that this is so means that the congregation must respect the uniqueness and freedom of the individual over against the collective of the
Church, and that there must be no kind of spiritual pressure or enforced conformity.

On the other hand, the individual Christian in all his uniqueness and
freedom can understand himself correctly only if he realizes that he is a
member of the whole body, and that he is linked to every other
member. The vertical relationship with Christ finds its fulfilment in its
awareness of the horizontal dimension of fellowship, that is, in its
awareness of the needs of the brethren and of the congregation as a
whole. The richness of the common service and the fellowship which
springs from it arises from this very fact, that it is not just a matter of
routine, but derives from the individual relationship of men and
women with Jesus Christ.

Finally we must note that the horizontal relationship is determined
as far as content is concerned by the vertical relationship. It is the latter
that contains what is essential, in that it represents the downward
movement of *agape*, which was manifest and active in Christ. *Agape*
means love and respect for the other despite his unworthiness, and
selfless, sacrificial service to him, to the whole body of Christ, and also
to the world. This means that the Church is essentially a fellowship of
love and service; and this is true for the individual, for the congregation as a group and for the Church as a whole. This service can be
fulfilled only when all share in its fellowship; yet at the same time we
must remember that no one can comprehend the full breadth of these
ministries and expressions of love inspired by Christ. It is our belief
that this love, as it becomes active and spreads through many hidden,
individual channels, has an influence in the world which far exceeds
anything we should suspect. But all these horizontal lines, along which
service is rendered in the power of Christ, can retain the nature of
agape only if they are rooted in and constantly nourished by that
fellowship of Christ with men which is bestowed in worship.

Seen in this light, we see that the Holy Spirit and *agape* are like the
two sides of the coin, though not interchangeable. They both represent
the essential gift which Christ bestows on the Christian, by which he is
now called to live. We shall not go far wrong if we link the two factors
as closely as possible and see the one in the light of the other. This helps
us to see immediately the significance of the Holy Spirit for the horizontal fellowship of the congregation in worship, and beyond it.
Whereas the human spirit erects barriers between men, sets them at a

distance from one another and thus isolates them, the Holy Spirit binds them together in all their multiplicity. He draws them together and creates mutual confidence by bringing them to believe in the fellowship, even when it is not visible. He establishes a new scale of values, for what is esteemed most highly is no longer individual human achievement, but the helpfulness which is born of love and the self-forgetful humility of serving others.

A fellowship, and a fellowship of service in particular, needs specific spheres of service if it is to develop to the full and not merely vegetate. For this reason, according to the New Testament, charismatic gifts are bestowed upon the congregation, which set the pattern for its worship and for its service within the Church and to the world. It is often lamented that one of the most obvious differences between the early Church and the Church of today is our apparent lack of charismatic gifts. At the same time, primitive Christian worship as we find it described in 1 Cor. 14, with its manifestations of the Spirit and of enthusiasm, makes us feel uneasy, and we prefer to be spared such fervent manifestations. This, however, involves a misunderstanding of the nature of the charismatic gifts which is harmful for our worship and for our common life, but which is the result of the particular form in which they appear in the New Testament. Here they appear as exclusively enthusiastic phenomena, such as we find occurring in many religions. From the point of view of the history of religion this is how we must describe the charismatic gifts in the New Testament. This external similarity to enthusiastic religiosity means that the recipients of the charismatic gifts are in constant danger of thinking of themselves and of the gifts bestowed upon them in terms of this kind of religiosity. When this happens the gifts become psychic powers more or less at the disposal of those who receive them. When they are thought of in this way, charismatic gifts become a serious threat to Christian worship, for the decisive factor is no longer God's service to us, but our human religiosity, by means of which we come to self-realization.

Paul does not attack charismatic gifts as such, for he recognizes that they are eschatological gifts of the Holy Spirit, but his main aim is to bring the recipients to a new understanding of themselves, and in particular to a new understanding of what they have received and of their task within the congregation. Paul helps the recipients to understand both themselves and their gifts christologically. The decisive factor in the gifts is not the enthusiastic element, but the eschatological. They are signs of the irruption of the Kingdom of God with its gifts of the Spirit and of love. In other words, they proclaim the coming Kingdom of Christ, and point beyond themselves and their recipients. They also bear witness to the immediate presence of salvation. The charismatic gifts are at one and the same time a gift and a task presented to the congregation by the *agape* of Christ. It is therefore not the element of the extraordinary that constitutes these gifts,[1] but the fact that they are the expression of the loving Spirit of Christ, by which He ministers to the congregation and its members.

As soon as we think of the charismatic gifts in the light of *agape* as the christological driving force of the congregation and the reverse side of the coin to the Spirit, and as that which makes the congregation a fellowship of service, the question of these gifts in relation to the Church of our day takes on a new aspect. These gifts need not by their very nature be linked with an enthusiastic religiosity, and can exist quite apart from it. If this is so, it follows that there have been charismatic gifts in the Church at all times, even though they have not always played the same part. The Catholic Church has taken account of them in its own way in its doctrine of the saints, by recognizing alongside the official ministrations of the Church a direct bestowal of the power of the Holy Spirit, of faith and of love. So long as this does not encourage an emphasis on works and on the merits of the saints rather than on Christ, then there is nothing to object to, although it would be a much simpler matter to look for charismatic gifts among ordinary Christians.

The New Testament gives us only a very general idea of what a charismatic gift is, and nowhere provides us with a definition. We can, however, pick out the following main features:

1. Charismatic gifts are eschatological gifts of grace bestowed through the Holy Spirit, which are not given to every Christian, but are a special gift imparted to certain individuals.[2] They bestow on the recipient special powers and authority in a particular sphere.

2. Those who receive the gifts face the particular danger of misinterpreting the gift bestowed on them as a private possession and of thinking of it as the expression of their personal power and authority. Instead of putting their gift to the service of the congregation, they then misuse it for enhancing their own importance. This implies that the charis-

---

[1] This point was made by Bultmann, *Theology of the New Testament*, I, pp. 160-1.

[2] All believers of course have the basic charismatic gift of the Spirit, which expresses itself in faith, love and hope; but over and above this there are "special charismatic gifts".

36

matic gifts are intimately related to the person of the recipient, and have in fact to be considered with reference to his natural gifts; but those without faith can easily misinterpret the charismatic gift as a talent, in other words as a natural endowment.

3. The only charismatic gift that can be recognized as such by the Church as edifying the congregation is that which, in accordance with its christological nature, is determined by *agape* and is dedicated to the fellowship of service within the congregation.

If we bear these three points in mind, we can go on in our attempts at definition to say that a charismatic gift has a twofold basis.

1. It is generally connected with some natural aptitude.[1] This natural "endowment", according to the principle *opera trinitatis ad extra sunt indivisa*, is a gift of the triune God. These God-given aptitudes are inherent in the man who is called by God, nevertheless they are a creation of the Spirit of Christ. However, He does not create from nothing; for just as the new man is not a *creatio ex nihilo* but a re-creation of the old, so neither can the Spirit fail to take natural aptitudes into account.

2. These aptitudes, however, would remain latent, or would be wrongly developed and used as talents for the personal advantage of the individual, if man were not endowed with the Holy Spirit through faith in Christ and called to service within the congregation. It is through the working of the Holy Spirit that the gift is either awakened and developed or first brought into the service of Christ and His people and thus completely changed.[2]

---

[1] On this point I am in full agreement with what Barth says concerning the grace-gifts in his *Kirchliche Dogmatik*, III, 4. Cf. p. 694: "What we see him doing as κλητός he does . . . at the new command and in the new power of God . . . in other words, he does it as something new, that completely transcends what he has been hitherto. But at the same time . . . it is *his* work . . . the work of this particular man, who both has his manhood behind him and also brings it with him, and in whose new name 'Paul' the old name 'Saul' is still preserved and is still recognizable."

[2] Cf. Barth, *op. cit.*, p. 721: "Even though the grace-gift as such is incomparably more precious than what may seem to him and to others to be his highest human endowment, nevertheless it is within the framework of his human endowment that the gift seeks to become effective. . . . It is hardly to be expected that the distribution of the different grace-gifts (1 Cor. 12; Rom. 12: 3 f.) should not stand in some relationship—at times an amazing relationship—to what these persons are in themselves. If there were no connection, how could we explain the fact that these people as bearers of these gifts had to be exhorted to recognize and express in practice their unity and their homogeneity in spite of all their

When we see the charismatic gift in this light, it becomes clear that although it is awakened by the Holy Spirit, it is not necessarily part of an enthusiastic religiosity. There are such gifts in our congregations, and there could be many more. There is no lack of talents in our day; what is needed is not enthusiasm, but faith and a love that is ready to serve, which will devote its talents to service for the sake of Christ, and thereby allow them to be transformed by the Holy Spirit.[1] From God's side there is the same opportunity for the unfolding of charismatic gifts as in New Testament times.

All this raises a question of our ordering of the Church and its worship, for in the New Testament charismatic gifts and the ordering of worship are closely linked. The Church and its worship are so flexible that the charismatic gifts as they emerge find their own spheres of activity, for it is only in this way that they can develop. Often we find that a charismatic gift is only recognized when an office is conferred upon a person and he accepts a sphere of responsibility of his own. The stimulus of responsibility and the spiritual demands that it makes awaken, and in a sense bring into being, what would otherwise never have come to expression. The question we must ask ourselves is whether we provide opportunities whereby such gifts of the Spirit, especially among the "laity", may be expressed in the life of our congregations, or whether this is hindered, if not actually excluded, by a too rigid ordering of the Church's life and worship. The life of the Church shows that where men are entrusted with offices, there charismatic gifts develop. But they need the opportunity to develop.

differences? We can explain this only if their human qualities, the personal aptitude and ability of each individual—which could easily prove to be all-too-human—are involved as well, only if the special purpose of the Spirit with each of them is revealed precisely in the capabilities and within the limits of each individual."

[1] We might take as an example the case of a young officer returned from the Forces, who is training for a new profession and who, in response to the Gospel, offers his services for youth work in the town in which he lives. In a short time his outstanding gifts for leading young people bring about a movement which attracts many students and infuses new life into the youth work of the Church. The young man, who could equally well have given his services to some sporting organization for young people, does not use his influence to make himself a "leader" or to achieve anything for himself. In the humility that springs from his relationship with Christ, he merely serves the cause and by so doing points directly, and even more indirectly, beyond himself to Christ.

38

II

THE SERVICE WE RENDER GOD IN WORSHIP

1. *Our service as response and co-operation*

WE REFERRED EARLIER to Luther's words in his Torgau sermon, to the effect that the purpose of worship is that "our Lord Himself may speak to us through His holy Word, and that we in turn may speak to Him through our prayers and hymns of praise".[1] These words helped us to distinguish the two sides of Christian worship, that is, God's activity and our activity, but it is not easy to define where the one ends and the other begins. The distinction we find in Melanchthon (*Apology,* XXIV) between sacramental and sacrificial elements in worship[2]—an unfortunate distinction to make—certainly brings out clearly the two sides of worship, but it has never been found possible in practice to arrange the component parts of the liturgy under these two categories. The reason for this is simple and obvious: that even in worship God speaks and acts not directly, but only through His Word and Sacrament, which He has committed to His Church and to individuals within it. God acts "in, with and under" the acts of His Church. It is through human speech that God proclaims His Gospel, and through human activity that He administers His Sacraments.

It is true that the Gospel was given to man. Christ brought it into the world and commanded that it should be proclaimed; but the apostles and the early Church, and Jesus Himself in fact, put this Word into human speech, so that it comes down to us through human testimony, which has provided the material for tradition. Again, it was Jesus who instituted the Lord's Supper, and it is His words of institution that are spoken over the elements; but these very words have come

[1] *Werke,* 49, 588.

[2] *Apology,* XXIV, 16: "The theologians rightly distinguish between sacrifice and sacrament. . . . A Sacrament is a ceremony or outward sign or work, through which God gives us that which the divine promise attaching to the ceremonies offers us. . . . On the other hand a sacrifice is a ceremony or work which we offer to God in order that we may honour Him." Kliefoth and Zezschwitz tried to separate the sacramental and the sacrificial actions in worship. Cf. Rietschel-Graff, *Lehrbuch der Liturgik,* I. 2 ed., pp. 48 f., esp. n. 5.

down in different versions, and it has fallen to the Church to determine the form of what is said and done in the action of the Lord's Supper, apart from the recitation of the *verba testamenti* and the use of bread and wine. Therefore both Word and Sacrament are at one and the same time God's service to us and our human service to Him. God's service to us and our service to Him permeate one another, and what God does for us He does only in, with and under our service.[1] This explains why those who attempt to describe worship are uncertain whether they should attribute preaching and the Sacraments to God's activity or man's activity in worship. In fact they belong to both sides, and we can therefore say that we have already considered both sides. But as there is considerable room left for man's activity, particularly in preaching and to a lesser degree in the Sacraments, and both have to be seen in the immediate context of worship as a whole, it seems right that we should include preaching and the Sacraments as we consider the human side of worship.

Most of the elements in worship reveal the same ambivalence. Even when they take the form of an address to God and a response from the congregation—as do the Creed, the prayers and the hymns—they are at the same time proclamation. They form a unity together with preaching and the Sacraments, so that we can say of the whole of worship that both sides interpenetrate to such an extent that it is impossible to separate them, although the Christian cannot but remain conscious of the difference between them.[2] God acts in, with and under the whole of Christian worship.

Many attempts have been made to define the relationship between the two sides of worship. K. F. Müller has tried to show, with reference to Karl Barth's christology, how the christological formula of Chalcedon, "without confusion and without change" but also "without division and without separation", can be applied to the doctrine of worship.[3] This formula helps to express the variety in unity and the unity in variety of worship, but the difficulty of applying the christological formula to the two sides of worship is that the relationship of

---

[1] P. Brunner, *Zur Lehre vom Gottesdienst der im Namen Jesu versammelten Gemeinde*, p. 192: "The two sides interpenetrate in the particular act of worship, as we saw from the example of the sermon and the Lord's Supper." P. 193: "In the Lord's Supper particularly God's gift and the offering of the congregation are bound in an indissoluble unity."

[2] P. Brunner, *op. cit.*, p. 193.

[3] See K. F. Müller, Die Neuordnung des Gottesdienstes, in *Theologie und Liturgie*, 1952, pp. 209 ff.

divine and human in Christ is a unique one, which is not reproduced either in the Church or its worship.[1] The human nature of Jesus, by its union with the divine, is free from sin. We obviously cannot draw this conclusion when considering the human side of Christian worship, for it is in constant danger of sinful perversion. It would be better to consider applying the formula *simul justus et peccator* to worship.[2]

The formula employed in Lutheran doctrine to describe the presence of Christ in the Lord's Supper, "in, with and under", has been used by Wilhelm Stählin in an attempt to set out the relationship between what God does and what man does in worship.[3] "In" expresses the fact that by the way He acts in worship and liturgy God does not despise our creaturely dependence on external forms, and thus underlines the idea of God's condescension. "With" reminds us that Christ really does participate in our human activities, without identifying Himself with them and without removing the creaturely imperfections from what we do. "Under" brings out the hiddenness of God's activity under human forms, which means that God's activity can be known only by faith. We have already used this formula to describe the relationship between God's activity and the service we render in worship because it expresses three important facts:

1. The complete penetration and inseparability of what God does and what we do in worship.

2. The fundamental qualitative difference between what God does and what we do in worship.

3. The vital importance of the service we render and of our task of discovering the best form for worship, if ever true Christian worship is to be offered.

Hebrews 13: 10–16 casts further light on the second of these three points. Whilst the use of the Chalcedonian formula seems to suggest

[1] Karl Barth has not used this formula to clarify the relationship between the two sides of worship. Cf. G. Harbsmeier, *Dass wir die Predigt und sein Wort nicht verachten*, pp. 70 ff.

[2] G. Harbsmeier, *op. cit.*, p. 78.

[3] Cf. *Formula Concordiae*, VII, in *Die Bekenntnis-Schriften der ev.-luth. Kirche*, II. 1930, p. 983; also W. Stählin, *Vom göttlichen Geheimnis*, p. 14. It is not easy to see why Harbsmeier (*op. cit.*, pp. 76 ff.) refuses to apply to the service of worship this formula, which was first used with reference to the Lord's Supper. It is also compatible with the principle *simul justus et peccator*. It is worth noting that Barth demonstrates what worship is by reference to the Lord's Supper. Cf. *The Knowledge of God and the Service of God*, p. 189.

that the two sides of worship correspond and stand in some kind of formal equality to one another, the truth is that the two sides are so different and correspond so little that it is questionable whether we should even speak of two "sides". Hebrews 13: 11, 12 speaks of the ministry of Jesus as High Priest against the background of all that has been said previously about this ministry. It is the unique and eternally valid self-sacrifice of Christ the High Priest, by which the world is reconciled and the people sanctified. All this is described as the activity of God, which is the foundation of Christian worship.[1]

The corresponding activity of man, which in this case means the congregation, is made up of three elements:

1. The call to go forth to Christ without the camp, which means leaving the securities of this world—which includes the cultic securities —and to bear His reproach. This involves an imitation of Christ which covers the whole of life.[2]

2. The reaction that is expressed in worship in the narrower sense is what is described in cultic terms as the sacrifice of praise to God, which has to be offered up continually. This is called "the fruit of lips" which make confession to God's name. We are not told whether this refers to proclamation, adoration or thanksgiving. The whole of worship therefore is response.[3]

3. In addition there is "doing good" and "communicating". We are not told whether "communicating" refers to the sharing of material goods or to the establishment and maintenance of personal relations in

---

[1] Cf. O. Michel, *Der Brief an die Hebräer*, 9 ed., 1955, in *Kritisch-exegetischer Kommentar über das N.T.*, edited by H. A. W. Meyer, pp. 344 ff., esp. p. 353: "In Hebrews the real sacrifice is the obedience of Christ, His suffering and His death; there is no further 'sacrifice' in addition to this that man offers. . . . It is possible, however, that the cultic idea is carried over logically from v. 10 to vv. 15 and 16." This last statement of Michel's is based on the assumption that the whole section from v. 10 to v. 16 is a unity.

[2] Michel, *op. cit.*, p. 347, holds that it cannot be decided for certain whether v. 13 refers to a separation from the world, as Chrysostom believed (a view maintained also by Windisch) or a separation from false doctrine. In any case v. 14 bears witness to the new age against the old.

[3] Cf. Michel, *op. cit.*, p. 351: "The early Christian service of worship takes place διὰ Χριστοῦ, i.e., through the mediation and in the presence of Jesus Christ. . . . 'The fruit of lips' refers to the hymns of thanksgiving that the congregation offers in place of animal sacrifices . . . the sacrifice of praise in heaven therefore corresponds to the sacrifice of praise on earth." It is not impossible to interpret v. 15 as referring to the Eucharist. "Great emphasis is placed upon prayer, upon the liturgy and upon preaching as the act of proclamation."

the assembled congregation. In any case the phrase "doing good" makes it clear that what is required is love.[1]

The response to God's act in Christ, therefore, is not only the cultic celebration of worship, for from man's side there is a threefold reaction: a total imitation of Christ, which means leaving the world behind, the proclamation of the Gospel and the performance of the liturgy to the praise of God, and finally love for one's neighbour in need.[2] To isolate the "cultus" as the sole response to God's act in Christ would be to abbreviate the response in such a way as to distort it. Worship can be a valid response to God's act in Christ only in the context of a total imitation and of the service of one's neighbour.

We must note that what is said concerning Christ on the one hand and man's activity on the other is expressed in a completely different terminology. It is true that in both cases cultic terms are used—in keeping with the whole trend of Hebrews—but the terminology used in each case brings out the qualitative difference between the two activities. We cannot even speak of the congregation's co-operation with what God does. Everything that the congregation does is reaction and response.[3] This is something that must be expressed, although in applying the formula "in, with and under" we have been emphasizing the inseparable permeation of the two sides. In principle the two sides must still be distinguished.

We shall see what this relationship is if we consider the "consecratory effect" of the *verba testamenti* in the Lord's Supper.[4] The celebrant cannot consecrate the elements by reciting the *verba testamenti*; he recites the words of institution in obedience to Christ's command and with the request for the fulfilment of the promise He made. The recitation

---

[1] Michel, *op. cit.*, pp. 353 f., tries to clarify the meaning of these two nouns, and their relationship to one another.

[2] Michel, *op. cit.*, p. 353, brings out the connection between them, showing that if one links together the different ideas and images in vv. 10-15 and considers them as having an inner unity, "the obvious thing to do is to look for liturgical connections behind these images. When we do this we find the beginnings of a new 'service of God'."

[3] *ibid.*, n. 2: "Sanctification, cleansing, forgiveness and perfection are in themselves *cultic* ideas, but in Hebrews they are thought of in the absolute sense as an *eschatological event.* . . . This eschatological event points to the heavenly and eschatological sanctuary. In view of the fact that Hebrews still thinks entirely in eschatological terms and recognizes only a heavenly cultus, it speaks of the Church on earth and of its life in a very unpretentious way and with little feeling" (M. Dibelius, *ThBl*, 1942, p. 11.).

[4] Cf. Vajta, *op. cit.*, pp. 182 ff.

of the *verba testamenti* by man is a proclamation of the real presence of Christ on the basis of His promise. It is by the grace of God that the proclamation and the realization of the presence coincide.

The difference between the two sides of worship brings out the fact that if God's activity is directed to the salvation of the world, then what corresponds to it is not merely the assembling for worship, important though this is, but the proclamation of the Gospel to the world and the turning of the world to Christ, which will not be completely fulfilled until the Parousia. In the light of this we see that the assembly for Christian worship must not lose sight of the world and all that is happening in it. Worship as man's response is therefore something very comprehensive, something that far transcends the liturgy, but which it must of course include. Here we see the justification of what P. Brunner says concerning the cosmological place of worship, and of his statement that the response to God's activity must be given not only by men, but also by the creatures and by the angels.[1]

In the light of all this, what significance can we attach to the human side of worship? One might feel inclined to describe this human side by means of the concept commonly used at the time of the Reformation, "*ritus* or *ceremonia*", but to do so might be taken as suggesting that this side is of no importance and has no meaning. It was not the intention of the Lutheran Reformation to suggest that ceremonies were of no importance when it distinguished between preaching and Sacraments on the one hand and ceremonies on the other, and described the former as necessary to salvation, but the latter as *adiaphora*. We have already seen that, despite the fundamental distinction, it is not possible to draw hard and fast lines between God's approach to us and our response, or between the sacramental and sacrificial elements in worship. In the same way, it is impossible to separate Word and Sacrament on the one hand and ceremonies on the other. For where do Word and Sacrament end and ceremonies begin? Attempts have been made to clarify the matter by drawing a distinction between form and content.[2] It is Christ's command that the Gospel should be preached and the Sacraments administered. The pure Gospel must be preached and the Sacraments administered as they were instituted (*Augsburg Confession*, VII). The way in which Christ's commands are carried out seems to belong to the realm of ceremonies, which are described as *adiaphora* (*Formula Concordiae*, X); but when it comes to the proclamation of the

---

[1] P. Brunner, *op. cit.*, pp. 168 ff.

[2] K. Barth, *The Knowledge of God and the Service of God*, p. 214.

pure Gospel, then form and content are closely related. And when we turn to the Lord's Supper, it becomes obvious that form and content cannot be separated, for the problem of form affects the content and in certain cases modifies it. The questions whether the *verba testamenti* should be spoken audibly, whether the Lord's Supper should be administered *sub utraque*, and whether the congregation communicates or only devoutly observes seem to touch only the form, but in fact concern the content as well.[1]

Thus we see that the distinction between Word and Sacrament on the one hand and ceremonies on the other, between the elements that are necessary to salvation and those that are *adiaphora*, is too crude and fails to take into account the intimate connection between form and content. In any case it would be a mistake to suggest that the problem of form is unimportant. Rather must we see—and we find this also among the Reformers—that the form of worship is a task with which the Church is faced. Fundamentally, the form is required to serve the content, which is the divine side of worship.[2] It must seek to point, as clearly and emphatically as possible, to the activity of God, which is the basis of worship.[3] It is the Church's task to find the form best suited to do this.

This task is a very varied and complex one. We can see this if we consider the motivation of the human activity in worship. Here we can distinguish three motive forces:

1. Christ's command to proclaim His Word and administer the Sacraments requires man's obedience.[4]

2. Man's own endeavour to find, by careful consideration, a form for worship that is appropriate to the activity of God. Such obedience is not merely a mechanical performance, but a responsible creative effort which opens up many possibilities.[5]

3. The spontaneous joy, which is the glad and free response to God's activity, and brings into play all human powers to His honour.[6]

---

[1] *ibid.*, p. 205.   [2] See P. Brunner, *op. cit.*, pp. 275 ff.

[3] K. Barth, *op. cit.*, p. 207: "On the contrary, the question we have to answer is how it might best correspond to its primary ground, the gracious will of Jesus Christ present and active in the midst of the Church."

[4] Barth does not go far enough in speaking only of obedience (*op. cit.*, p. 206). Christ allowed the Church a greater freedom by laying down only what was essential.

[5] See H. Asmussen, *Die Lehre vom Gottesdienst*, p. 120.

[6] See R. Guardini, *The Spirit of the Liturgy*, pp. 96 ff., and E. Schlink, *Zum theologischen Problem der Musik*, 2 ed., pp. 13–20, 24.

The combined effect of these different motives—which of course are not experienced as distinct motives—has been to produce a variety of liturgical forms. E. Schlink has pointed out how the different structures of the various theological declarations have left their mark upon the life of the Church and in particular upon its worship. He considers prayer, praise, witness, teaching and the confession of faith and compares the particular form of these statements with statements of a different structure, and comes to the conclusion: "Only in *all* the basic types *together* can *the whole* of what has to be said in response to the Gospel be said, only thus can a worthy reply to God be given; to restrict the responses of faith to just one of these types would mean an impoverishment not only of form, but also of content, and, what is more, disobedience to God."[1] Therefore the Church is required in the arrangement of its worship to pay attention not only to the content, but also to the correct structure of the service of worship, which corresponds to what the Church believes. This structure can never claim that its particular form is necessary to salvation or that it alone conforms to the content of worship, for it will always be contingent and to some degree inadequate. Nevertheless it is the task of the Church by exercising its responsibility and its freedom to discover the most adequate form.

Whether our worship is a true service of God in obedience to His command and in response to His act in Christ, or whether it degenerates into a perverted cultic performance, depends, theologically speaking, on whether we determine correctly the relationship between what we do and what God does in worship. We should not be able to offer worship at all if it were not for the fact that God desires our response and our co-operation and only requires that we should respond with the free spontaneity of faith and with childlike trust. The worship that springs from faith is prior to the theology of worship, for it is a spontaneous growth. The critical function of theology is that of subsequently inquiring whether worship is performing its appointed task.

2. *Preaching, the Sacrament and the liturgy*

Our aim in this section is to examine the Sunday services we hold in our Churches, against the background of what we have already discussed concerning the nature of worship. We cannot attempt to give a historical account of the development of worship or of its separate

[1] E. Schlink, Die Struktur der dogmatischen Aussage, in *Kerygma und Dogma*, 1957/4, p. 262. (My italics)

parts, nor can we discuss the course of a service in detail. We cannot attempt to describe the most desirable form of worship to be aimed at either, but can only try to cast some light upon its structure and by so doing give some guidance for the arrangement and conduct of a service.

It has long been recognized that it is a denial of the very nature of worship, to think of it as an artistic production built on rational or psychological lines, although since the Enlightenment many attempts have been made to develop worship along these lines.[1] We need only consider the process by which Christian worship developed, a process lasting over a century and a half, to see that this is a wrong approach.[2] Worship, as we see it in the basic pattern of the Mass, which is reproduced in all the great liturgies of the Church,[3] can be compared to the medieval cathedrals, which in the course of the centuries have been altered and extended, but have grown into structures which, full of contradictions and yet all the more significant for their purpose, point beyond themselves.[4] Protestant liturgical scholars were right in opposing the tendency in the Protestant Churches particularly at the beginning of this century for the minister to impose on the service a psychological or thematic pattern of his own choosing.[5] Some, however, went too far in the other direction by refusing to re-examine the structure of the liturgy, suggesting that one should accept without criticism or examination the loose juxtaposition of the various elements as something given. Catholic liturgical scholars, not having to contend with the psychological and thematic whims of individuals, have sought to bring out the main elements in the structure of the service and thus draw up a fixed order.[6]

Recently Protestant scholars also have given more attention to the problem of the structure of worship. Here we may mention the valuable examination of the "basic forms of theological declaration" by

---

[1] P. Graff, *Die Geschichte der Auflösung der alten gottesdienstlichen Formen*, II. pp. 39, 51.

[2] J. A. Jungmann, *The Mass of the Roman Rite*.

[3] G. Dix, *The Shape of the Liturgy*, 3 ed., 1947, pp. 36 ff., 103 ff.

[4] J. A. Jungmann, *op. cit.*, I, pp. 2 ff.; T. Klausner, *Abendländische Literaturgeschichte*, 1948, p. 3.

[5] H. Asmussen, *op. cit.*, pp. 194–203; C. Mahrenholz, Preface to *Entwurf der Agende für die Ev.-luth. Kirche und Gemeinden*, I, 1, 1951, pp. 23–27. J. Kulp, Die Kollektengebete, in *Der Gottesdienst an Sonn- und Feiertagen*, 1949, pp. 285–93, opposes any attempt to distinguish the separate parts of the liturgy.

[6] J. Pascher, *Eucharistia*, Gestalt und Vollzug; J. A. Jungmann, *op. cit.*, I.

E. Schlink. H. Asmussen, O. Cullmann and P. Brunner had previously explored this field. Schlink discusses the theological declaration and casts light on its structure. When we consider together the various forms of declaration we see that of the four mentioned by him, three are directly concerned with the sphere of worship.[1] It might be better, therefore, to speak of them as basic liturgical forms. If we adopt this approach, it becomes possible to see congregational worship in the light of the basic elements in its structure, which gives us valuable theological insights into the offering of worship.

The main *basic elements* in all Christian worship[2] are preaching, the Sacrament and the liturgy.[3] We are not using liturgy here in its wider sense, as embracing the whole of worship, but in the narrower sense in which it describes the order of worship with the exception of preaching and the Sacrament. We do not intend to examine in detail each of these basic elements, but rather to consider their relationship to one another. Each of these three elements has its own structure and function in worship, but there are important connections between them.[4]

Preaching and the liturgy have this in common, that they employ only the Word, in contrast to the Sacrament with its use of material elements linked with the Word. The Sacrament and the liturgy are alike in that they are both actions in the performance of which both celebrant and congregation play their part, separately and together, thus introducing into worship the element of event and movement. By contrast, preaching consists only of speech. In the Sacrament and the liturgy the Word is fixed and is repeated at every time and place, but in preaching the Word is free, and is determined only by its adjustment to the particular situation. Finally, preaching and the Sacrament

[1] Cf. E. Schlink, *Die Struktur der dogmatischen Aussage*, pp. 251 ff.; H. Asmussen, *Die Lehre vom Gottesdienst*, pp. 100–186.

[2] Cf. O. Haendler, *Grundriss der praktischen Theologie*, 1957, section 13, p. 159. Haendler also speaks of the elements in a service of worship, but they are quite different from those we have in mind. He draws them from the phenomenology of religion, not from the Church's confession of faith.

[3] Cf. H. Schlier, *Die Zeit der Kirche*, 1956, pp. 224–64. To a certain extent we can find these basic elements already in Acts 2: 42, if we interpret "fellowship" as "contributions", that is, the collecting and distributing of goods and money. (Cf. E. Haenchen, *Die Apostelgeschichte*, 1956, p. 157, in Meyer's *Kritisch-exegetischer Kommentar über das N.T.*) W. Löhe speaks of the "component parts" of a service, and comes to the same conclusions (*Der evangelische Geistliche*, II. 1958, p. 168).

[4] As originally only the Lord's Supper was a regular element in the service, and Baptism was administered during it only in exceptional cases, we shall restrict our observations to the Eucharist.

go together as being expressly instituted by Christ and commanded to be continued by His Church. They differ from the liturgy also in that they are the primary channels through which the promised presence of Christ is given. It is the will of Christ to come among His people through preaching and through the Lord's Supper.

It is here that God's service to us and our service to Him are most directly linked, and it is God who effects the link. The fact that in both these instances Christ is in a special way serving the congregation finds expression in the Lutheran Church in the fact th   as a rule public preaching and the administration of the Sacrament are restricted to the ordained minister commissioned by the congregation. Thus in this function the ministry can be said to represent Christ Himself. By contrast, the liturgy is performed by the minister and the congregation alternately. It takes the message and the promise contained in preaching and in the Sacrament and unfolds them. In principle any part of the liturgy may be taken by the congregation or by a part of the congregation, either by a liturgical choir or by an individual who represents the congregation, such as a reader or one who leads the prayers. The liturgy can therefore be said to be the basic element in every part of worship, in which the congregation (consisting always of minister and congregation) comes to the fore. It is in the liturgy that it makes its own response to the activity and gift of God in preaching and in the Sacrament, a response which is made freely and yet at the same time in a set form.

We can now see how all these three basic elements are related to one another. However, they still do not lose their distinctiveness, and in fact they can fulfil their various functions in the service only if their own particular character is clearly expressed. The function of preaching, together with the Sacrament, is to keep clearly before our eyes the movement from God to the congregation. There is no room here for evoking a religious atmosphere or stimulating a pious mood in the congregation, for its task is to proclaim the saving act of God in Christ, on the basis of the Word of Holy Scripture.[1] In contrast to the Sacrament, it shares with the liturgy its verbal character, and is not tied to the narrow limits of the Sacrament, which leave little room for individuality and freedom. Its task is not only to keep alive the Biblical message, but so to assimilate the Word independently that its message can be presented afresh out of one's own understanding and with originality and imagination. In contrast to the liturgy, therefore,

[1] Cf. K. Barth, *Church Dogmatics*, I, 1, pp. 70 ff.

preaching does not expound a "timeless" doctrine in "timeless" ecclesiastical language, but applies this doctrine as directly and concretely as possible to the immediate situation.

Whilst the liturgy includes the congregation in its action, with the result that it enters into the dialogue and develops its own initiative in giving its own response to the Gospel, preaching requires the congregation to listen. But this does not mean that the congregation is inactive. According to Barth, "In the Church to act means *to hear*, i.e. to hear the Word of God, and through the Word of God revelation and faith. It may be objected that this is too small a task and one that is not active enough. But in the whole world there exists no more intense, strenuous or animated action than that which consists in hearing the Word of God."[1] Hearing is different from singing. One of the troubles with people today—even within the Church—is that they can no longer listen, for it means ceasing from every external activity and holding oneself still and prepared like a ploughed field in springtime ready for the seed. With such receptiveness the sermon can make its impact upon the congregation; and the sermon in its turn will help to create such receptiveness.

The Sacrament also needs this fertile receptiveness, but the sermon appeals more to man as a conscious being,[2] whereas the Sacrament makes its appeal more strongly to the unconscious, and even to the physical, part of man. We might go so far as to suggest that each of the main elements in worship lays claim to one organ in particular by which man maintains contact with the outside world. In the case of preaching it is the ear, which gives access to man's reason and will.

The Sacrament also brings the congregation to an attitude of faithful receptiveness towards the gift which God offers and to which we ourselves can add nothing. The Sacrament consists of Word and elements. In contrast to preaching, the Word is reduced to the barest minimum, consisting of two or three sentences which contain the essence of the whole Gospel. The reaction to Word and elements, and to the gift conveyed thereby, is different from the reaction to preaching. Although the intellect may not be passive, a man does not so much receive with his ear, but rather tastes and feels. The Word is conveyed to him, as it were, materially through the sign. It always denotes a deviation when objection is taken to the fact that the Sacrament is a material sign and the attempt is made to spiritualize or intellectualize it, as all

[1] K. Barth, *The Knowledge of God and the Service of God*, p. 210.
[2] K. Barth, *Church Dogmatics*, I. 1, pp. 151 ff., H. Schlier, *op. cit.*, p. 259.

enthusiasts have done. The result has always been to deprive worship of the sacramental element, thus always preventing its proper development.

The Sacrament and the liturgy are particularly closely associated, for by its very form the celebration of the Sacrament is necessarily liturgical. Therefore the Sacrament has in common with the liturgy a traditional language, which has been the language of the Church for generations and is not that of any particular individual. By means of these unchanging and constantly repeated phrases a man, conscious of the transitoriness of his own life, experiences the continuity of worship through many generations and the all-embracing fellowship of the Church. As it is a question in the Sacrament of the activity of God and our reception, there is less room here for the spontaneity of the congregation than anywhere else in worship. In the eucharistic liturgy almost every word is fixed. The *ordinarium* determines the whole action in the "canon" and in the communion, the *proprium* having only a small place in the preface and in the final collect. This does not prevent the Sacrament from being an action in which the congregation takes part.

In so far as the celebration of the Sacrament is liturgical, it shares the dialogue character of the liturgy. But at the heart of the celebration of the Sacrament are two factors which distinguish it from the rest of the liturgy: on the one hand the *verba testamenti*, which are the words of consecration, and on the other hand the distribution together with the words of administration. The *verba testamenti* used as the words of consecration are, as we saw earlier, to be thought of as the proclamation and repetition in obedience of Christ's words of institution and as a request for the fulfilment of the promise of His presence.[1] In both cases the eucharistic liturgy is, as it were, interrupted, and this is inappropriately expressed in the Roman liturgy by reciting the *verba testamenti* inaudibly. There is no response from the congregation to the words of divine comfort expressed in each instance, apart from the response of hearing and receiving as in the case of the Word. Only God acts, and in what He does the words of institution and the communion are most intimately connected. It was for this reason that Luther wanted to bring them together at the same moment in his *Deutsche Messe*.[2] The special nature of these two phrases underlines their direct connection with the elements. The words of institution and of administration and

---

[1] V. Vajta, *op. cit.*, pp. 182 ff.
[2] *Werke*, 19, 99.

the action of the Sacrament are inseparably linked. In addition we must note that, in contrast to preaching which addresses itself to all, the distribution is to the individual, and also that, in contrast to the liturgy in which the congregation acts and reacts, in the Sacrament it is silent and passive. The Sacrament makes its inescapable impact upon each man as a person, and he is merely the recipient.

Luther rightly felt that this aspect of the Sacrament, which springs from the very essence of the Gospel, had been not only obscured, but destroyed, by the great act of prayer which the Church offers, for the Church has expanded the celebration of the Lord's Supper (from the offertory to the canon) and constantly overloaded it with new words and actions, often of a fanciful kind. We might go so far as to say that the Sacrament was turned into liturgy, and what was the act of God alone was turned into an act of the Church and of the priest. Luther was therefore right in discarding all the liturgical ballast in order to lay bare once again the basic structure of the Sacrament, even though in the process some things of value may have been lost.

The liturgy shares with preaching its verbal character, but it is also active in character, like the Sacrament, It appeals at the same time to the ear, the touch and the eye. The word in the liturgy is different, therefore, from that in preaching. It is primarily a fixed Word, though there are various degrees of fixity. It takes the form of dialogue, which is in keeping with its active nature, and dialogue requires short, polished phrases, which can be readily understood. As the liturgy is the communal response of the congregation, unfolded by means of a conversation between it and the minister, the congregation must be able to play a vocal part. The minister should appear only as a partner, and it should be possible on occasion for his place to be taken by a member of the congregation. In arranging the order of worship as much room as possible should be left for the initiative and spontaneity of the congregation.

The liturgy, as a result of its growth through the centuries, is a complex structure, and we must look more closely at this structure if we are to understand the liturgy and pass a judgment on it. Just as worship as a whole is composed of various basic elements, so also the liturgy for its part is made up of certain basic forms which can be further divided into special types. Schlink discusses these forms,[1] and distinguishes four that are basic: prayer, praise, witness and teaching.

[1] E. Schlink, *op. cit.*, pp. 251 ff.; see also H. Asmussen, *Die Lehre vom Gottesdienst*, and P. Brunner, *Zur Lehre vom Gottesdienst*, pp. 194ff., 283 ff.

This list, however, is not complete, for it omits the basic form of blessing, which covers salutation and formulas used in absolution, consecration, Baptism and benediction. It could also be argued that the announcements should be considered as a separate form, but they should
probably be reckoned with preaching as they refer to the immediate
situation, to the actual life of the individual members of the congregation as a whole, and of the Church and society.[1]

As we are concerned not with theological statement, but with
worship, we can also modify Schlink's two basic forms "witness" and
"teaching", the former of which refers primarily to preaching and the
latter to theology, and draw a distinction between "witness" and
"reading". From the synagogue onwards reading has been an important basic form in worship—though not in theological statement—
and is subject to different laws from preaching.[2] Both must be given
their place in worship alongside each other. They cannot be substituted
for each other, for they are complementary. We find that reading
played an important part even in the worship of the early Church. It
expresses the voice of the apostolic Church and turns men's attention
to the saving acts of God as recorded in the Old and New Testaments.
It is particularly at Passiontide that reading should come to the fore. It
is not without significance that the accounts of Jesus' sufferings, death
and resurrection are so predominant in the Gospels. Evidently they
were narrated in the worship of the primitive Church, very soon in a
set, unchanging form.[3] It appears that the story of the Passion was
narrated as a continuous whole, and in later times it was read in the
same way.[4]

A service in which the readings are neglected for the sake of the
sermon is in danger of placing too one-sided an emphasis on the person
of the preacher and of making his views more important than those of

---

[1] H. Asmussen, *op. cit.*, pp. 242 ff.

[2] See G. Kunze, Die Lesungen, in *Leiturgia* II, pp. 161 ff.

[3] See M. Dibelius, *From Tradition to Gospel*, pp. 22 ff., 178 ff.

[4] G. Schille shows in his instructive article, Das Leiden des Herrn. Die Passionstradition und ihr "Sitz im Leben", in *ZThK*, 1955, pp. 161–205, that there must
have been different traditions of the Passion, and suggests "that the Passion
tradition in the Gospels derives from the celebrations, in particular the Easter
celebrations, of the primitive community" (p. 198). He recalls the question posed
by L. Fendt: "In the time of Matthew and Luke, who used readings like the
Passion story—and where?" (*ThLZ*, 1953, p. 328). Schille goes on to say "that
the community kept alive the remembrance of Good Friday and Easter in its
annual celebrations", at which long sections of the accounts were read aloud.

Scripture. On the other hand, a service in which the Word is re-presented by reading alone, which is allowed to supplant the free proclamation through the sermon, loses the quality of direct application and fails to make the sacred text live.

It is only recently that it has been recognized that the Reformation brought not only preaching, but also reading, to its proper place at the centre of worship. "The Reformation brought about a change which was far-reaching and of lasting consequence, by reading the Gospel not merely in its traditional place as *one* element among the other propers, but by making it also the text for the sermon. From then on the Gospel, which for too long had been neglected, begins to penetrate and determine every part of the principal service of worship. . . . Thus Michael Praetorius, from the standpoint of Church music at the beginning of the seventeenth century, could describe the Gospel as the *caput et principale* of worship."[1] The Gospel reading becomes the dominant factor in the whole Sunday liturgy.

We can say, therefore, that in the liturgy the following five basic forms stand side by side:

1. Prayer, which takes the form of the confession, the introit psalm, the collect and the intercession; to some extent the hymn, especially the Agnus Dei, can be included here; and finally, extempore prayer and the Lord's Prayer.

2. Praise, which is expressed in the congregational hymn, the Gloria, the Hallelujah, the Creed and the Preface, and also in the eucharistic prayer and the doxology at the end of the Lord's Prayer.

3. Reading in its various forms.

4. Preaching, or witness. Some hymns come under this heading.

5. The formulas of blessing, which were enumerated above. The Amen is not easy to classify: does it come under praise, like the end of the Lord's Prayer, or is it to be included in the category of witness as being an affirmation of the witness given, or again should it be taken to be a formula of blessing?

Worship has grown in the course of the Church's history. Its basic forms are present from the first in the liturgy, and there is not one of them that could not be traced back to the New Testament.[2] These

---

[1] *Ordnung der Predigttexte*, edited by H. Beckmann, W. Metzger, and C. Mahrenholz, 1958, pp. 5, 9.

[2] Cf. G. Delling, *Der Gottesdienst im Neuen Testament*, pp. 50–136, and E. Käsemann, Liturgische Formeln im Neuen Testament, in *RGG*, 3 ed., II, 993 ff.

basic forms have grown along with worship. In the Middle Ages a rampant growth set in which on the one hand pushed preaching to one side and on the other obscured the true nature of the Sacrament, as enshrining what God does for us, by means of a spurious liturgical form, which nevertheless was made up of two genuine basic forms: that is, the prayer of consecration which is a combination of prayer and blessing. Prayers are addressed to God and blessings to man, giving him an assurance of the grace of God; but we find arising prayers which are almost magical, and which seek to influence the way God acts and to heighten their effect by their multiplication. It is at this point that Luther intervenes and excludes all such prayers in the offertory and the canon of the Mass.

Luther saw clearly what were the three basic elements in worship, and sought to let them fulfil their function. He also restored the basic forms of the liturgy according to their true nature. As a result worship could once again fulfil its task, and in the order drawn up by Luther the basic elements which, though obscured, were still present in the Roman Mass, stood out again in their true light.

The first part of the service puts the emphasis on prayer, understood in a sense wide enough to include adoration. This part lasts until the collect, which closes this section of prayer. The salutation before the collect introduces a different element and foreshadows the next section, but we cannot go into the questions of liturgical history that this raises.[1] The second part of the service has at its centre the proclamation of the Word, in the form of the readings and the sermon. The announcements also belong here.[2] The service concludes with the Sacrament, in which the main liturgical elements are those of blessing and praise. When we remember that prayer is the basic form of the congregation's response to God's activity and is also therefore the basic form of the liturgy, we can say that the free play of these liturgical forms, combining in various ways, makes its influence felt in every part of worship. What we find therefore is not a logical, nor even a psychological, structure.

[1] See J. A. Jungmann, *The Mass of the Roman Rite*, I, pp. 361 ff.

[2] The Creed, which comes between the readings and the sermon as part of the service of the Word, was not inserted until later, when the sermon had already been moved from this part of the Mass and placed at the beginning. The Creed thus marks the transition to the sacramental section (cf. Jungmann, *op. cit.*, I, pp. 461 ff.). It belongs not to the Mass of the catechumens, but of the believers (*ibid.*, p. 474). By placing the Creed between the reading and the sermon we tend to think of it as an act of proclamation rather than as an act of praise.

What Schlink says in regard to the Church's statements of faith can also be applied to worship: "Only in *all* the basic types *together* can the whole be said. . . ."[1] To restrict the response of faith to just one of these types would mean an impoverishment not only of form, but also of content, and, what is more, disobedience to God, for it would mean refusing fully to recognize His saving acts and the fullness of the divine revelation that they convey."[2] As far as the service is concerned, this means that room must be allowed for the three basic elements of worship and the five basic forms of the liturgy.

If we are to give as complete a picture as possible of the structural elements in a service, there is a further aspect to be considered, namely, that there are three sections to be co-ordinated: the *ordinarium*, the *proprium* and the free elements. The expert will probably be surprised at the mention of this third factor, for the only distinction normally drawn is that between the *ordinarium* and the *proprium*, between the part that remains constant throughout the Church's year and thus forms the framework of the liturgy, and the part that changes according to the season. We can see this from the structure of the offices, where the free elements are not laid down, and therefore do not appear in the service-books.[3] This disregard of the free elements is no doubt the result of the influence of the Catholic approach to worship, in which preaching is not on the same level as the Sacrament and the liturgy. As far as Protestant worship is concerned, however, this presents a distorted picture of worship. Preaching occupies a place of such significance that it cannot be ignored in the structure of a service.

Unfortunately there is no appropriate Latin term for what I have called the "free elements". Such a term would have to correspond to the other terms *ordinarium* and *proprium*, and also bring out clearly what it stands for over against what the other two sections have in common. The free elements are that part in an act of worship that in its wording neither can nor should be planned or laid down beforehand in the order of service, but must be left to the responsible initiative of the one appointed to conduct the service, as something to be done afresh each time within the framework of the set order. In a service therefore there is this polarity between the parts that are already formulated and laid down by the Church and are to be performed everywhere in the same way, and the parts that the officiant formulates for

[1] E. Schlink, *op. cit.*, p. 262. (My italics)
[2] *ibid.*, p. 263.
[3] See C. Mahrenholz, *op. cit.*, pp. 20 ff.

a particular service, for a particular congregation and in a particular situation. To express it differently, we could say that whilst the *ordinarium* and the *proprium* have to be performed in a service, as something laid down in advance by the Church, the free elements are carried out on his own initiative by the person officiating in the service. To omit these free elements would turn the service into a mere lifeless repetition, as happened to a large extent to the mumbled masses of the Middle Ages. The combination of prescribed and free elements helps to prevent the *ordinarium* and the *proprium* from becoming mere repetition, and gives new life to them each time they are repeated responsibly. On the other hand, a service consisting only of free elements, such as we find among enthusiastic sects, lacks this element of repetition, and also the element of the Church's continuity.

Luther was aware of this polarity, without expressing it in such terms. The idea, however, plays an important part in his liturgical reforms. The clearest expression of the necessity of this polarity is given in *Von der Ordnung des Gottesdienstes in der Gemeine* (1523).[1] His main objection to the Roman services is "that God's Word has been stifled, and merely read or sung in the churches, which is the most serious abuse". Luther demands that the lessons should be not only read, but also expounded: "Afterwards the preacher, or whoever is appointed to do it, should stand forth and expound part of the lesson, so that all the people may understand, learn and be admonished. The first requirement, that of reading the passage out aloud, is what Paul calls in 1 Cor. 14 'speaking with tongues'. The second requirement is that of interpreting or prophesying and speaking with the spirit or the understanding. Where this is not done, the congregation is not edified by the lessons, as happened in the monasteries and convents, where the lessons merely echoed round the walls." Luther sums up by saying: "The important thing is that everything should be done to this end, that the Word may have free course, and that it should not be turned again into the moaning and droning such as prevailed before."

Luther's main concern, of course, is that the Gospel should be proclaimed intelligibly, so that it can be understood and believed. But such proclamation requires, over against the prescribed liturgy with its responses, readings and collects, a free exposition and a living preaching; in other words, all that is meant by *viva vox evangelii*. It is like a living fire which makes the cold lava of the liturgy glow again. According to Luther there can be no worship without this element of

[1] *Werke*, 12, 35 ff.

freedom. It is an essential component in a service. This does not mean that a set liturgy is to be rejected: on the contrary, in the work from which we have been quoting Luther gives detailed instructions concerning the readings from Scripture, the psalms and responses, etc., in the various weekday services. Over against the lifeless Roman rite, however, all the emphasis is on "giving the Word free course".

This brings to the fore once again an element that has affected the structure of Christian worship from the New Testament onwards, but which at the same time concerns more than its structure: the fact that its liturgical form must be kept open to the Holy Spirit. In the New Testament we find side by side a liturgical terminology, which has apparently already attained a fixity of form as a result of the repeated performance of the liturgy, and an immediacy in those filled with the Spirit and in the evangelical preaching which breaks through all fixed forms. It was inevitable that in the first generations the free, direct element should predominate over the fixed element; and it is important for Christian worship at all times that it should contain not only parts that require to be repeated on lines that have been followed for centuries, but also parts that demand a direct spontaneity. It is here that the man who, through his faith in the Word, feels urged by the Spirit, can and must give free rein to the Spirit's urge. "Quench not the Spirit" (1 Thess. 5: 19). The living voice of proclamation which is heard in this way gives new life to the set liturgy, and at the same time reminds it that there is nothing final about it. The set liturgy, on the other hand, reminds the living voice of proclamation that it is subjective and limited by circumstances, and links it with the witness and confession of faith of the whole Church.

Schlink makes this same point:

By their very nature the intercessions and the sermon, especially the evangelistic sermon, are freer from a set form of words than are teaching, confession of faith and praise, for in the intercessions the immediate situation is laid before God, and the witness of the sermon also has its bearing on this immediate situation. Important distinctions arise in the individual structure of theological statements according to which of the elementary responses of faith are tied to a set form of words (e.g. whether it is confession of faith or preaching, intercession or praise) and according to the extent to which these set forms of expression supplant or prevent the free statement of belief. . . . A fixed response and a free response go together in just the same way as the believer can accept the Gospel only in the fellowship of believers, but at the same time he can do this only as a unique individual, who discovers himself

58

only as he responds to the love of God. It is only by the correct combination of fixity and freedom in the declarations of its faith that the Church shows its identity and continuity through all the ages, and that it still maintains this identity and continuity as it goes on constantly making its impact upon new realms by its witness. . . .[1]

There are two other items to be considered at the same time as the sermon. The extempore prayer at the end of the sermon has become less and less common, which is to the loss of worship. It can be considered as the logical conclusion of the sermon. The term "collect", although it has long been used for a different type of prayer, best expresses what is needed at this point, for this prayer sums up all that the sermon has awakened in the congregation by its proclamation of the Gospel—a sense of sin, thankfulness, adoration and concern. Another free element in the service is the announcements.[2] Since the Enlightenment the Protestant Churches in Germany have forgotten the significance of the announcements.[3] They are an important yardstick for measuring how concrete is a congregation's sense of fellowship and responsibility for each of its members, for the congregation as a whole and for the problems of the Church in the world. It is worth taking note how the announcements are made in the Protestant Churches in the United States, for they are in fact an important part of the worship of the congregation, and are not just an element in its structure but express something of its content.[4] It is also worth remembering that

[1] E. Schlink, *op. cit.*, p. 264.

[2] See H. Asmussen, *Die Lehre vom Gottesdienst*, pp. 242–48.

[3] See P. Graff, *Die Geschichte der Auflösung der alten gottesdienstlichen Formen*, II, pp. 138 f. We should do well to take to heart the words of Mahrenholz (*op. cit.*, p. 40): "The place of the announcements is a particularly controversial matter in the ordering of worship. One point we must not forget: the mentioning by name of members of the congregation for whom intercession is to be made, the reference to events such as baptisms, weddings and funerals that affect the life of the congregation, the indication of the purposes to which the collections are devoted, and the mention of happenings that are important for the life of the Church—all this is an organic part of the service, and has its rightful place there as a piece of genuine and natural worldliness. To exclude it from worship would indicate a dangerous spiritualizing tendency and an unhealthy 'solemnity'. In spite of all the pseudo-liturgical patterns we must assert that in Christianity we cannot isolate the life of worship 'inside' from the life of the Christian 'outside'. It is worth noting that the New Testament letters, which were of course read out in the service of worship, do not end in the style of a hymn or sermon, but with prosaic personal observations."

[4] There are of course some aspects of the announcements in the North American Churches that cannot be recommended for imitation.

many of Luther's sermons lead on without the break of a final Amen into the announcements, which are an application of the message proclaimed. We often find in Luther that sermon, announcements and extempore prayer form a unity.[1]

To sum up, we can say that the trilogy of the *ordinarium*, the *proprium* and the free elements is an indication of the temporal setting of Protestant worship. The *ordinarium*, which always remains constant, links it with the "dimension of eternity"; the *proprium* links it with the Church's year, which, as it follows the course of Christ's life, at the same time bears witness to the course of the Church through the world to the Kingdom of God; and the free elements, which take account of the immediate situation, bring the present moment into the Church's worship. In other words, the background of eternity, the message of Christ and the actual life of the congregation are all brought together in the service of worship.

3. *Worship and the life of the congregation*

One of the results of recent developments in theology and in the understanding of the Church is that almost all those who are concerned with these matters agree in the view that worship is the centre of the Church's life. There is a sound theological basis for this view, as a result both of the findings of New Testament scholars and also of the careful re-consideration of the nature of worship. The Liturgical Movement, together with the revival of hymn singing, and the fact that it was around worship that the Confessing Churches in Germany drew closer together during the Church Struggle, have helped to bring new life to our services. In many services the congregation is taking part to an extent never known before. It is taking its share within the liturgy, groups from the congregation are taking parts of the liturgical chant, and individual members are playing an active part in the service as readers or by performing other functions. The renewed liturgy and the Protestant hymn book have transformed the singing of the congregation. Among those in our congregations who realize that they share a responsibility for the Church's worship there is slowly growing up the understanding that liturgical questions should be settled theologically and not primarily according to the criterion of feeling, or from the standpoint of merely maintaining what is traditional.

[1] See A. Niebergall, Die Geschichte der christlichen Predigt, in *Leiturgia*, II, p. 272.

Nevertheless in many places worship is still far from being the centre of the Church's life. Statistics of Church attendance show that attendance at worship has not declined, but these figures represent only a fraction of the nominal members of the Church.[1] Still more serious is the fact that our services are often a stumbling-block rather than a source of strengthening even for the most loyal members of our congregations, on account of the dullness of the preaching, the lack of fellowship and the unsatisfactory liturgical form which makes it impossible for those present to play their proper part in the liturgy. Although we have emphasized that God's saving activity in and through worship and the fellowship created by worship are objects of faith and not of sight, and that this tension between what is believed and what is seen must be affirmed and accepted, the fact remains that we must constantly seek to discover what we can do to make worship more effectively the centre of the Church's life.

Let us consider first what the minister, as he tries to bring his people to worship, can do as regards himself and his ministry. From all that we have said so far there emerges a very elementary fact, which is almost too simple to state and yet is so far-reaching that much depends on it. It is that the minister must begin from the fact of what God is seeking to do in Christ in a particular congregation. In other words, he must look at worship and the congregation with the eye of faith instead of with the eye of reason and doubt. He must believe that in Christ God has acted decisively for these people, that it is Christ's will to be present and active in this congregation through Word and Sacrament, to create fellowship within it and to equip it for service. The minister must never lose sight of this divine activity, which far exceeds what we ourselves either attempt or see. In all that he does he is merely God's workman, who prepares the materials. The important thing is what God Himself does. This conviction gives the minister certainty, peace of mind and patience. It also gives him an unequalled resilience when faced by set-backs.

This certainty, that God is acting through Word and Sacrament and is thereby building up His people, provides a centre around which the minister can organize his work. The work of many ministers suffers from the fact that it has no centre of gravity or a false centre of gravity. The abilities and charismatic gifts of different people lie in different spheres, and ministers are no exception to this rule. Nevertheless, the centre of their ministry should always be the Sunday worship. One can

[1] See J. Beckmann (ed.), *Jahrbuch für die EKiD*, 1954, p. 341.

tell from a service whether the minister, because of the pressure of other duties, has left its preparation to the last minute and is conducting it as a matter of routine, or whether he realizes that it demands the full force of his faith and his ability. To have this centre of gravity helps the minister to distinguish readily between what is essential and what is non-essential. There are many who spend their days as managers doing work of which others could relieve them, whilst they neglect the essential work to which they are appointed. This essential work is the spiritual and intellectual preparation for worship. The two must go together: on the one hand asking for the gift of Christ's ministry through Word and Sacrament, and on the other hand striving to understand the message and to give shape to the sermon he feels he must preach in the light of the text and of the situation of his congregation.

This twofold preparation for worship should run through the minister's whole week like an invisible thread. Exegesis, quiet, thoughtful meditation on the text, and the effort to give shape to the sermon are all necessary if the sermon is to come to gradual fruition. A careful division of one's time makes it possible to leave room for these things even in a very full time-table. On the whole it is true to say that in the Church we run the danger of over-organization: we do not do too little, but rather too much, and often not the right things.[1] This urge to do too much—just as the resignation that leads to idleness—springs from a lack of faith in the activity of God: because He is not doing it, we must do it, and yet we do not achieve it. We may allow ourselves to be deceived for a time by the activity created by the organization we have set in motion, and we may even for a time mistake such activity for life. But whatever we have done, and not God, will always come to naught.

The minister who sees his congregation with the eye of faith will not make the mistake of confusing the limits of God's activity with the limits of his own work, for example, with attendance at the services he conducts or sharing in his organizations, or with the various expressions of faith for which he is responsible. It often happens that ministers who do their work with great ability and devotion regard those who for various reasons cannot take part in the work of the congregation as outside

---

[1] Cf. the words of Präses D. Wilm at the Westphalian Synod in 1955 (printed in *Verkündigung der Kirche heute*, II, p. 82): "It is not in the first place a question of works, but of faith. The call therefore is not to do more, but to believe more. For where faith is, there love and service and works follow."

the fold. They overlook the fact that God can reach people beyond the reach of our activities, that such people may refrain from active participation in the life of the congregation for reasons that are important and acceptable to God, and also that it is possible to serve God in one's calling and in the world. Therefore it is quite wrong for a minister to feel in his Bible study group, for example, that here is the true Church, the *ecclesiola in ecclesia*, or when there is a full Church at a Confirmation or at Christmas for him to give vent to his annoyance with those members who do not come to Church on any other occasion. When he does this he is drawing distinctions which only God knows and which He alone has the right to draw.

Such an egocentric attitude endangers both worship and preaching, for to look at everything from the standpoint of one's own work is to leave God out of one's reckoning. It also means setting up a barrier between oneself and those outside, by refusing to put oneself in their place and treat their problems and temptations seriously, with the result that one cannot speak the helpful word encouraging them in their faith that springs from the solidarity of standing together in the trials of life. There is nothing more important for the minister who wishes to make worship the creative centre around which the life of a Church revolves than that he should take into account the activity of God, which is far greater than anything we can do.

There are many things in the arrangement and outworking of the Church's life that can be made to bear witness to the fact that worship is its creative centre. The first problem that arises is whether the congregation is to be divided into groups or split into "cliques". Division into groups is necessary, and in fact we find the New Testament speaking of the Church as a body with various members. We should not interpret members here as referring only to individual Christians, but also to the groups within the Church. In the New Testament we see a grouping of the Church into old and young men, into widows and young women (Acts 5: 6; 1 Tim. 5: 1 ff.; Tit. 2: 1 ff.; 1 John 2: 12 ff.). This kind of grouping is even more urgent in these days of vast communities, although of course there are other reasons for it as well. It is impossible to establish in large city Churches inter-relationships between all the members either through their attendance at worship or through the pastoral visitation of the minister. It is impossible to establish such relationships between all the members, and the most we can hope to do is to establish them between some of them. The principle that must be applied is that of *pars pro toto*: the relationship that a member has to certain other Christians in the Church is representative for him of the fellowship he has with the whole congregation.

It is desirable of course that large parishes should be split up and new smaller ones created in order to make congregations of reasonable size. But we must not forget that further division is limited by the number of available ministers and the financial resources of the Churches. Some kind of division into groups is essential in a Church's life. Whether the groups are based on distinctions according to sex or age, on cultural interests (musical, educational, dramatic, etc.) or on neighbourhoods will be determined by local circumstances. It is a matter that requires insight and initiative, imagination and adaptability on the part of the minister and his fellow-workers.

Whether a congregation is divided into natural groups or split up into "cliques" depends on two factors:

1. If a group lives by worship, directs all its activities towards it and realizes that it is a responsible member of the body, then it is a true member. But when a section breaks away from worship and builds up its own life alongside that of the congregation and becomes self-sufficient, then there is a danger of its becoming a "clique".

2. If a group is prepared to hear the call of the Gospel to service, which may involve many different kinds of service, then it is a true member of the body. But when it becomes so self-sufficient that it refuses to serve or persists in maintaining services which, though they were once justified, are now no longer required, whilst there are other services in the Church that are waiting to be performed, then it has cut itself off.

For a healthy Church life it is necessary to overcome this splitting up into "cliques" in favour of a natural division into groups. It would be a mistake, however, simply to destroy the "cliques", for one would run the risk of being left with a completely atomized body. A section which is not prepared to acknowledge its responsibility to the whole body, and which has proved itself to be sterile, can be left to die a natural death. The majority of such "cliques" arose from the various associations that were a feature of the nineteenth century, but which have now disappeared as a result of social change. It is often possible to form new groups which are genuine component parts of the Church. Looser groups, formed for a specific purpose, are more appropriate in our present situation than the more rigidly constituted associations of an earlier day. The difficulty of such groups is simply that they are unstable because their members are unwilling to commit themselves to a particular service. For this reason they often do not reach the point where they develop their own offices and their own leadership, which means that the leadership falls again on the minister. This weakness afflicts those groups particularly which never go beyond discussion to practical service. What such groups want most of all is someone with whom they can enter into theological conversation without committing themselves, which is why they become so dependent for their very continuance on the co-operation and initiative of the leader. Such groups also feel that the link with the worship of the congregation is best provided through the person of the minister, who plays an active part as leader or as a member of the group.

Out of their concern that all these groups should be linked with worship as the centre of the Church's life, and to prevent possible aberrations under lay leadership, many ministers think that they are indispensable in these organizations. Whilst fully recognizing the practical difficulties that constantly arise, we must nevertheless affirm that in so doing the minister is failing to take full account of the activity of God, which cannot be identified with his own activity. God seeks to act through many members of the congregation in many different ways, and it is necessary in full confidence to allow laymen opportunities for the development of their own responsibilities. We may recall what was said earlier concerning the development of charismatic gifts in our congregations and of the need for providing adequate opportunity for them. Lay responsibility has to be learnt, and has to develop its own tradition. When this happens, there will appear the spiritual gifts which can both relieve the minister and also bring a new wealth of gifts and life to the congregation. Such lay responsibility can grow only where there is a brotherly collaboration between laity and ministry.

We must now go on to consider how the congregation can be brought to understand the significance of worship. It has been recognized for a long time that the catechetical ministry of the Church should be linked far more closely than it has been in the past, and than it is even now, with the worship of the congregation. The instruction given even to young children should be first and foremost a training for worship. Many recent manuals point in this direction. In this respect we have something to learn from the Catholic Church.

If children are to feel at home in worship it is especially important that they should take part in the service with their parents from an early age. The question that arises here is whether we should have a children's service, or whether the children should take their place in the worship of the whole congregation. The latter alternative is possible only where, following the American pattern, the children take part with their parents in the liturgy of the congregation and leave before the sermon to go with their teachers into the church hall for instruction in groups. When it is a preaching service without the Sacrament the children return to the service after their classes or after the sermon; but when the Sacrament is being celebrated, they have their own concluding prayers and can then play until the sacramental service is finished.

Such a scheme presupposes of course that there is a church hall where the children can be taught whilst the service is in progress, a playground where the children will not disturb the sacramental service, and that there are teachers who are willing to be absent from the sermon and the Sacrament at the principal Sunday service. Where these prerequisites are not present, the scheme we have outlined is not possible. It is important that these matters should be borne in mind when new church buildings are being planned. To bring children into the liturgy of the adults can awaken a deeper understanding of worship at an early age and can effect an easier transition from children's worship to the worship of the whole congregation; it keeps the family together on Sunday morning and saves mothers of small children the worry of leaving their children unattended. Against all this we must set the danger of demanding too much of the children, and the danger of the disturbance they may cause by their presence in the service.

All the various groups within the congregation should realize that they are anchored in the Church's worship. There is a limit, however, to the direct and active part which they can take as separate groups, apart from those who are concerned with the musical side of worship. What is important for these groups is that they should not stand out in worship as separate entities, but be willing to be just a part of the congregation.

On the other hand it is possible to link the activities of many organizations directly with worship or to form special groups to prepare for it. There are some churches where the lesson on which the sermon is based is discussed in advance in the elders' meeting or in the men's, women's or youth organizations. The aim of such groups is to help the minister to make his message relevant to the actual problems in the day-to-day life of his congregation. There are also groups which meet to discuss the sermon after it has been preached. Their task is to bring out the full meaning of what they have heard and by considering it together to try to find ways of applying it to the actual life of the members. Finally there are prayer groups which prepare for worship. A much more indirect way of linking the life of the groups within the Church with worship, which is nevertheless very effective, is to observe the Church's year. A group which reads the Sunday lessons at its meetings and practises the hymns for the services or makes itself familiar with the liturgy is living in the rhythm of the Church's year, which is also the rhythm of the Sunday worship.

The opportunities for giving laymen particular tasks to perform in a service are limited in our form of worship. It is easiest of all to appoint people to take the collection. It is much harder to obtain collectors for house and street collections! The office of reader, to which falls the reading of Scripture in the service, requires thorough training if this part of the service is to retain its proper function in worship. Services consisting of readings which are taken by laymen need even more thorough preparation. An office which is common in the United States, but is not really established amongst us, is that of stewards who welcome people and show them to their place. The young people of the congregation should be brought together far more than hitherto to form a choir which has its part in the liturgy and if possible its place in the choir stalls. It is obvious that our type of worship with its emphasis on preaching and the Sacrament allows only a limited sphere of activity in the Church's worship to individual groups within the congregation. This is not just a weakness, but also an indication of the fact that in worship all the various groups must learn to be simply the congregation and realize that the awareness of belonging to a particular group must give way to the awareness of being part of the congregation.

The supplementary services provide special opportunities for allowing laymen to play an active part in worship. Evening services, services to mark the close of the week and the services during Passiontide afford opportunities to some groups within the Church to take over the responsibility and take the part not only of the choir, but also of the reader or the officiant. The possibility of addresses being given by selected speakers from such groups should also not be ignored, where there is evidence of ability. I know of one Church where each evening during Holy Week various speakers from a different group within the congregation read the Passion story from a different Gospel or from a harmony of the Gospels as part of the Passiontide services.

Finally we must note a practice that has developed and proved effective in the United States: that of a systematic invitation to people to come to worship, undertaken by members of the congregation. Special training is given to those who engage in this kind of service, who devote much time and energy to the task of visiting people outside the Church, whose addresses have been supplied by other members of the congregation. The method they employ is to call on Sunday morning on people they have previously visited and accompany them to Church, and then to visit them again later after they have taken part in a service and discuss any questions that may have been raised, try to overcome any opposition there may be and help them to link themselves with the congregation. It would make a great difference to our Church life if we could persuade our laymen with professional experience to undertake a similar service.

To what extent should the usual arrangement of our services be adapted to changing social circumstances? The Church must be flexible as regards the time of its services. As a general rule it should not change what is the time of Sunday morning service in almost all the Protestant Churches in Germany, that is, between nine and eleven o'clock. But it ought to provide short services at different times, according to local circumstances. For example, early services might be considered, which would be particularly convenient for housewives who have no help in the house, or services on Sunday evenings during the summer when many take the advantage of a five-day working week to go away from the towns at the week-end. In industrial areas the fact of shift-work should be taken into account in arranging the times of services.

Such an increase in the number of services would, of course, mean a heavier burden for already over-burdened ministers, particularly as regards preaching. This argument holds good, however, only so long as the present pattern of the ministerial office is considered the only possible one. If we compare the number of our services with the number of services held in the Church at the time of the Reformation, or even with the number of Masses celebrated in Catholic Churches, we shall see that there has been a very great reduction. It might be a good thing for our Churches, and also for our ministers, if there were more services; but this would be possible only if there were no increase quantitatively in the minister's duties. To avoid this, his duties in other spheres would have to be rigorously reduced. Many administrative responsibilities, for example, could be taken over by laymen. Sermon preparation need not demand more time, as it is better to repeat one well-prepared sermon on the same day than to deliver a number of indifferently prepared ones. If such repetition is not possible, for reasons which we cannot go into here, then we must re-learn the art of preaching short sermons which concentrate on expounding one central thought contained in the text.

At every period in the history of the Church a certain duration has been considered reasonable for a service, determined not so much by the nature of worship as by the general feeling concerning time in the particular period. At the time of the Reformation it was felt that sermons should not last longer than three quarters of an hour. Luther often complained that Bugenhagen failed to observe a time-limit in his preaching.[1] In the Age of Orthodoxy, on the other hand, sermons lasted up to two hours. The age in which we live has a keen sense of time. It lives by the clock, and is prepared to allow only important speakers to disregard the time factor. There is no theological reason why one should not exercise the discipline of setting oneself a time limit in the service and in the sermon. Anyone who cannot say all that is necessary in 20 minutes will not do it in 35 minutes either. He either has nothing to say, or does not know how to express himself with precision. We must learn to preach with brevity, and yet with substance, on the principle *multum non multa*. We shall not train our congregations to listen again until we learn to convey much matter in a short space of time, in the way that is expected in public life and on the radio.

We have spoken earlier of the basic elements in the liturgy and of the basic forms in the service as a whole. We need mention now therefore only two items, which bring out the link between the congregation and its worship. These are the announcements and the taking of the collection, which ought to be considered together. The announcements should not be allowed to become a mere catalogue of Church activities. Room should be made for news of families belonging to the congregation.[2] This of course is easier to do, and it has more significance, in small communities than in very large ones; it can help to break down the anonymity of the members of the congregation, especially if the minister can add a personal word of encouragement to the people concerned. This practice can also give the congregation information which will suggest subjects for prayer. The announcements therefore can lead to common intercession in the service—

---

[1] See Luther's *Table Talk*; cf. Clemen. VII, pp. 27, 2643a; 35, 5171b.

[2] See C. Mahrenholz, *op. cit.*, p. 40.

which is why the best place for the announcements is in the pulpit, following the sermon—and also to private intercession. Finally, the giving of the congregation would be set free from the mechanical nature it generally has if the minister could bring home to the congregation the purpose for which its money is given. We have understood for a long time that money plays an important part not only in the life of society, but also in the life of the Church, and therefore it cannot be ignored in the service. But we have not yet drawn the liturgical consequences of this fact.

An important and much discussed problem today is the question whether the Church should take its services out of the Church building and try to establish, in centres of modern industry and business, communities based on various trades and professions with their own services.[1] Such services for individual professional groups are nothing new. Outlines of services drawn up specially for miners are already in existence.[2] Despite the altered social circumstances of today, we can still learn from what has been the practice of the Church for centuries. It has ministered to every trade and profession that has requested it with its message, and also with special services and devotions, and it should do the same today. In doing this in the past, however, the Church has never neglected the worship of the congregation as the principal service. This idea of the "principal service" is quite justified. In contrast to the services held by separate groups and sections of the community, the worship of the whole parish is still the principal service. The argument against the parish as an outmoded ecclesiastical and sociological unit is itself now outmoded, as with the rapid spread of the five-day week and of automation the family has more time to itself and business and industry no longer make a total claim upon a man. As a result the community in which people live gains a new importance.

We might note two facts that point in this direction: firstly, that the Communist party before its dissolution in West Germany was transferring its main efforts from the centres of industry back to the areas where people live, and secondly, that over half the citizens of West Germany are house owners or own a piece of land, or are saving to

[1] H. D. Wendland, *Die Kirche in der modernen Gesellschaft. Entscheidungsfragen für das kirchliche Handeln im Zeitalter der Massenwelt*, 1956, pp. 149, 220 ff.; E. zur Nieden, *Die Gemeinde nach dem Gottesdienst*, pp. 48 ff., 59 ff.

[2] Cf. G. Heilfurth, Gottesdienstliche Formen im beruflichen und betrieblichen Leben des Bergbaus, in *Verantwortung für den Menschen*, edited by F. Karrenberg and J. Beckmann, 1957.

build a house of their own. However, important though these factors are, they are not theological arguments. What is important from the theological point of view is that the Church has to offer the Word of God everywhere and to everyone who desires it, but at the same time it must not lose sight of the fact that worship and congregation belong together. The local congregation, which includes both men and women of all ages and all professions, is best fitted to lay hold of modern man in the wholeness of his existence. This is not to say that the limited part that the communities in business and industry can play is unimportant.

In conclusion we must mention the question of the introduction of the so-called full order of worship. By this we mean a service, such as we see in Justin as early as about the year 150,[1] in which the sermon and the Lord's Supper are combined in the framework of the ancient order of the Mass. If it is correct that there are three basic elements in a service, preaching, the Sacrament and the liturgy, then all three are indispensable. This supports the re-introduction of the full order of worship. However, we must not delude ourselves about the history of Christian worship, and in particular about the fact that apart from the first centuries there has been no period in which preaching and the Sacrament received equal emphasis. In the ancient Church the sermon was very quickly displaced in favour of the Sacrament and the liturgy, and this state of affairs continued through the Middle Ages. Luther restored the full order of worship by putting the sermon once again at the centre alongside the Sacrament; but even in his lifetime people in Wittenberg were leaving before the Lord's Supper and had to be exhorted to remain for the Sacrament.[2] Thus the emphasis immediately shifted to the sermon, at the expense of the Sacrament. The conditions for a general introduction of the full order of worship in the average congregation are far less favourable in our busy and distracted age than at the time of the Reformation. That was a time of strong religious feeling and conviction, which is more than can be said of the age in which we live.

Wherever circumstances permit, the full order of worship should be observed. This is probably possible more often than we imagine. It should be easiest to introduce it in small Church fellowships which meet for a special purpose, and also in small congregations and at conferences. Where it is felt that the full order could not be introduced as

---

[1] Justin, *Apology*, I, 65 and 67.
[2] See P. Graff, *op. cit.*, I, pp. 177 f.

it would demand too much of the congregation, one could either hold a service with the Lord's Supper every four weeks, or celebrate the Lord's Supper immediately after the main service, inviting the congregation on each occasion to take part.

Even if we cannot now reach the ideal of all three basic elements being given their place in every service, it is important that they should all be given their due emphasis within the various services that make up the life of the congregation.

In all our discussion of the structure and conduct of worship we must never forget that everything we do from our side is our human response to the service that God Himself renders us, a service He renders "in, with and under" what we do. It is this Divine activity that makes worship the centre of the Church's life.

Let us recall once again in closing what happens in worship. We can do no better than quote the comprehensive description of what faith perceives as taking place in worship, from the *Ordnung des kirchlichen Lebens der Vereinigten Evangelisch-Lutherischen Kirche Deutschlands*, which is printed as a preface to the *Agende für Evangelisch-Lutherische Kirchen und Gemeinden* (1957).

> In worship the congregation assembles by God's command and promise, in order to have the assurance in Word and Sacrament of the presence of its Lord. Wherever the Word of God is truly proclaimed in its purity and the Sacraments are administered in accordance with Christ's command, the Lord is present and active in all His grace. It is here that the Holy Spirit summons, assembles, enlightens, sanctifies and maintains the Christian community. It is also here that the congregation confidently brings its prayers of petition, intercession and thanksgiving before the triune God and adores Him in His majesty. It praises God in its hymns and offers Him its sacrificial gifts. This whole activity, governed by the Word of God, is called liturgy.
>
> In its worship the congregation transcends all divisions and is united with the community of Christian people of all times and places, and with the company that is before the throne of God. In the midst of the world it awaits the coming of its Lord.

BIBLIOGRAPHY

I. ON THE HISTORY OF WORSHIP

Bornkamm, G.   Herrenmahl und Kirche bei Paulus, *ZThK*, 1956/3.

Bornkamm, G.   *Jesus von Nazareth*, Stuttgart, 1956. (E. T. *Jesus of Nazareth*, London, 1960.)

Bultmann, R.   *Theologie des Neuen Testaments*, Tübingen, 1948. (E.T. *The Theology of the New Testament*, vol. 1, London, 1952; vol. 2, 1955.)

Cullmann, O.   *Urchristentum und Gottesdienst*, 2 ed., Zürich, 1950. (E.T. *Early Christian Worship*, London, 1953.)

Delling, G.   *Der Gottesdienst im Neuen Testament*, Göttingen, 1952.

Dibelius, M.   *Die Formgeschichte des Evangeliums*, 2 ed., Tübingen, 1933. (E.T. *From Tradition to Gospel*, London, 1934.)

Georgiades, T.   *Musik und Sprache, Das Werden der abendländischen Musik*, Berlin, 1954.

Graff, P.   *Die Geschichte der Auflösung der alten gottesdienstlichen Formen in der evangelischen Kirche Deutschlands*, vol. 1, 2 ed., Göttingen, 1937; vol. 2, 1939.

Jungmann, J. A.   *Missarum Solemnia*, 2 ed., Vienna, 1949. (E.T. *The Mass of the Roman Rite: Its Origins and Development*, vol. 1, New York, 1951; vol. 2, 1955.)

Lansemann, R.   *Die Heiligentage, besonders der Marien-, Apostel- und Engeltage in der Reformationszeit, betrachtet im Zusammenhang der reformatorischen Anschauungen von den Zeremonien, von den Festen, von den Heiligen und von den Engeln*, Göttingen, 1939.

Rietschel, G.   *Lehrbuch der Liturgik*, 2 ed., revised by P. Graff, Göttingen 1951–2.

Schmidt-Lauber, H. C.   *Die Eucharistie als Entfaltung der verba testamenti.* Eine formgeschichtlich-systematische Einführung in die Probleme des lutherischen Gottesdienstes und seiner Liturgie, Kassel, 1957.

Stählin, R.   *Die Geschichte des christlichen Gottesdienstes von der Urkirche bis zur Gegenwart*, in *Leiturgia*, Handbuch des evangelischen Gottesdienstes, vol. 1, Kassel, 1952.

Zimmermann, U.   *Die Preussische Agende im Rheinland und ihre Auswirkungen bis zur Gegenwart*, Düsseldorf, 1956.

II. ON THE THEORY AND PRACTICE OF WORSHIP

Asmussen, H.　　*Gottesdienstlehre*, vol. 1: Die Lehre vom Gottesdienst, Munich, 1937.

Barth, K.　　*Gotteserkenntnis und Gottesdienst nach reformatorischer Lehre,* Zollikon- Zürich, 1938. (E.T. *The Knowledge of God and the Service of God according to the Teaching of the Reformation,* London, 1938.)

Barth, K.　　*Kirchliche Dogmatik,* IV. 1, pp. 718 ff.; IV. 2, p. 722 ff., 790 ff., Zollikon-Zürich, 1953, 1955. (E.T. *Church Dogmatics,* IV. 1, pp. 643 ff.; IV. 2, pp. 638 ff., 697 ff., Edinburgh, 1956, 1958.)

Brunner, P.　　Zur Lehre vom Gottesdienst der im Namen Jesu versammelten Gemeinde, in *Leiturgia,* vol. 1, Kassel, 1952.

Guardini, R.　　*Vom Geist der Liturgie,* Ecclesia Orans, vol. 1, Freiburg, 1922. (E.T. *The Spirit of the Liturgy,* 1937.)

Hahn, W.　　*Gottesdienst und Opfer Christi.* Eine Untersuchung über das Heilsgeschehen im christlichen Gottesdienst, Berlin, 1951.

Harbsmeier, G.　　*Dass wir die Predigt und sein Wort nicht verachten,* Munich, 1958.

Mahrenholz, C.　　*Entwurf zur Agende für evangelisch-lutherische Kirchen und Gemeinden,* vol. 1: Vorwort und Ordinarium, 1951.

Müller, K. F.　　Die Neuordnung des Gottesdienstes in Theologie und Kirche, in *Theologie und Liturgie,* Kassel, 1952.

Nieden, E. zur　　*Die Gemeinde nach dem Gottesdienst,* Stuttgart, 1955.

Rendtorff, T.　　*Die soziale Struktur der Gemeinde.* Die kirchlichen Lebensformen im gesellschaftlichen Wandel der Gegenwart, Hamburg, 1958.

Pascher, J.　　*Eucharistia.* Gestalt und Vollzug, Münster, 1947.

Pope Pius XII.　　Encyclical *Mediator Dei,* 1948.

Schlink, E.　　Die Struktur der dogmatischen Aussage als ökumenisches Problem, in *Kerygma und Dogma,* 1957/4.

Schlink, E.　　*Zum theologischen Problem der Musik,* 2 ed., Tübingen, 1950.

Stählin, W.　　*Vom göttlichen Geheimnis,* Kassel, 1936.

Vajta, V.　　*Die Theologie des Gottesdienstes bei Luther,* Göttingen, 1952. (E.T., condensed, *Luther on Worship,* Philadelphia, 1958.)

Wendland, H. D.　　*Die Kirche in der modernen Gesellschaft.* Entscheidungsfragen für das kirchliche Handeln im Zeitalter der Massenwelt, 2 ed., Hamburg, 1958.